The
POWER
Process

An NLP Approach

To Writing

By

Dixie Elise Hickman
&
Sid Jacobson

Published by The Anglo-American Book Company,
Bancyfelin, Carmarthen, Wales.

First published in the UK by

The Anglo-American Book Company Ltd
Crown Buildings
Bancyfelin
Carmarthen
Wales

First published 1997.

British Library of Cataloguing-in-Publication Data
A catalogue entry for this book is available
from the British Library.

ISBN 1899836071

Printed and bound in Wales by
WBC Book Manufacturers,
Waterton Industrial Estate,
Bridgend, Mid Glamorgan.

Table of Contents

List of Figures

Acknowledgments

We give special thanks to Glenn E. Oehms, who developed the POWER SPACE model, and to the many students, workshop participants, and corporate clients over the years who have helped us develop, fine-tune, and verify the usefulness of the ideas in this book.

No book on NLP is complete without acknowledgment and thanks to Richard Bandler and John Grinder, co-developers of the ever-expanding technology of Neuro-Linguistic Programming. Their genius, collective and individual, has seldom been matched in the field of human behavior and systems thinking. The same goes for Leslie Cameron-Bandler, Judith Delozier, the late Todd Epstein, David Gordon, especially for his work in the craft of metaphor development, and Robert Dilts, who is responsible for many of the useful NLP ideas in this book, including the Neuro-Logical Levels.

Thanks, too, to the folks at Anglo-American, for their care for details and their persistence through technological difficulties.

Individually, Dixie adds her appreciation to her family for their support and encouragement, especially husband Glenn Oehms, daughter Kyla, and parents, Mac and Billy Hickman, and to Sid for his collaboration and efforts in finding the right home for this book.

Sid gives special thanks to his wife and long-time companion Cindi Jacobson for putting up with him all these years and to his parents, brothers, in-laws, nieces, nephews, and other extended family, for the same reason. Permanent appreciation is extended to Dixie and Glenn for their contributions and hard work in making this book, and the ideas in it, a reality.

Sid also thanks and acknowledges the intelligence and collective talent of the writer's group he participated in for several years: guide, writer, and poet Kay Murphy, poet Laura Miller, Denise Chetta, Brian Hannon, Dr. John Willis, and his closest and dear friend of many years, Claudia Barker. Some of these have since published some truly beautiful work. He hopes to continue in that vein.

Preface To POWER

Another book on writing? Will this one be any different from the others? Yes. And yes, this one has something the others are missing. *The POWER Process*? The title of this book isn't just a catchy phrase meant to sell books. It's a reflection of the techniques we'll teach you. We aren't promising you fame or fortune. We do promise to get you writing better, faster, easier and more often. By the way, you'll have more fun, too.

WHAT THIS BOOK IS ABOUT

The POWER Process works; we know it does. This model has been tried and proven consistently. We began with analyzing the writing process of successful writers, people who are effective and efficient, and discovered some important elements they had in common. We compared their patterns with those of people who have trouble writing. Then we distilled out the necessities in the process, packaged them in a form easily taught and learned, and gave it to others. Their improvement in writing has shown us how well we have done.

What you won't find here are rules of grammar, sentence diagrams, and other standard fare. Nor will you find invention techniques and artificial writing assignments. We assume you already have something to say, and you want to say it better. That's why you picked up this book. What you will find here are methods for improving your own thinking processes, getting in touch with the skills and talents you have, and making better use of the "rules" you already know.

HOW THIS BOOK DIFFERS FROM OTHERS

There are things in this book never before included in any book on writing, as well as new combinations of more familiar things.

First on the list of differences is Neuro-Linguistic Programming (NLP for short). Essentially, NLP is a model of human communication. It was developed to study the elements of excellence itself, regardless of the subject or activity. It gives us the tools to build the best possible model(s) of anything that works well. We use NLP in everything we do. It guarantees our effectiveness.

Second is a simple, but not oversimplified, model of what to do when you write, a model based on what effective writers actually do and how they use their thinking processes while they do it. Drawing on current research in the processes of writing and creativity, we go beyond those models using the tools of NLP, and package the result so that you can use it. Best of all, although you will be using the same thought processes as truly effective writers, you will be able to maintain and even enhance your own personal style.

Third, this book will actually get you writing as you go through it, step by step. No matter how incapable or how stuck you think you are, we'll guide you through the same steps that create successful results for others, and you will create them as well. These steps take place inside your head and in your behavior, as well as on your paper or your word processor. And the process is self-reinforcing in nature. It feeds on its own success. So as you step through the workbook experiments, use the material you are actually working on—or wish you were working on. This book will help you unlock your creative juices and release the power of your ideas.

Fourth, while this is primarily a book about writing, you will find yourself applying these principles and techniques to other areas of your life. You may even surprise and delight yourself as the learning from this book automatically expands into other parts of your thinking and behavior.

Fifth, these new styles of thinking you learn will not only get you writing but will also teach you a lot about yourself and people in general. Writing is a very personal thing, and anything that makes you a better person can make you a better writer.

Finally, you will be building enjoyment into the learning and writing process. When you enjoy what you are doing, you learn it faster, do it more, do it better, and want to do it again and again. That doesn't mean we'll take all the work out of writing. Good writing will still take time and effort. But it can also be a lot of fun.

HOW TO USE THIS BOOK

This book is designed so that you can read it at your leisure, use it as a workbook to actually guide yourself through a writing project, and keep it handy as a reference guide for handling special problems or situations.

There's a second Preface in **Part I: POWER Sources** that describes our ethics and attitudes toward you. Then the next two chapters give you a general overview of what we'll be working with. *The Context of POWER* introduces our model of the writing process. It also explains why many writers run into writing blocks; it's very easy to lose awareness of the complete context of your writing. *The Power of NLP* explains some techniques for using your brain more effectively and gets you started on using it to write more effectively.

The next four chapters in **Part II: The POWER Process** take you step by step through the POWER process. We'll introduce you to some other writers who have solved their writing problems using our methods to make their writing more comfortable, more streamlined and more effective. Then we'll guide you in using these methods as you step through the process with your own writing project. These exercises will literally install effective writing strategies in your thought processes, both conscious and unconscious, and in your behavior. You will learn to elicit your own best states of mind for certain tasks and train yourself so that you can get into the proper frame of mind when you want to.

Part III: POWER Applications deals with special kinds of writing and how the POWER process can be applied or adapted to such situations as literary writing (fiction, poetry, and drama), business correspondence, and school papers. In the **Appendix** you'll find extra worksheets, answers to the most common questions and problems people have with writing, and a streamlined quick-reference guide through the POWER Process. And finally, there's a brief bibliography for more specialized concerns and for further exploration of NLP.

Although we recommend starting at the beginning and reading and working on through with a specific writing project, you may want to go ahead with the first two chapters while you decide how you want to apply it first. Or you may want to work on several projects at the same time. However you begin, this is a book to be used—and enjoyed. So read on, and more POWER to you!

Part I

POWER Sources

Chapter One

Preface To
Neuro-Linguistic Programming

Neuro-Linguistic Programming was developed in the early 1970's by Richard Bandler, Ph.D., an information scientist, and John Grinder, Ph.D., a linguist. It grew out of their research into the structure of influential communication, at the University of California at Santa Cruz. Early studies were conducted on the communication styles and techniques of extremely powerful psychotherapists. Later the inquiries were expanded into a wide variety of other fields. Through this study of highly successful people, Bandler and Grinder discovered common patterns of behavior that made people effective in their chosen field.

This *Preface to NLP* explains some of the philosophy behind the technology and the assumptions on which it is based. You may, if you're very impatient to begin writing, save this section for later reading. But if you're wondering about what kind of tools we'll be using and about the attitudes of the authors toward you, here is some insight into our basic beliefs.

The technology, or methodology, of NLP is human modeling—building models of how people perform or function in different endeavors. It is also based on an attitude that anything that anyone can do can be duplicated by others. The combination of this attitude and methodology creates applications and techniques on a continual basis. NLP is full of practical applications needed by everyone—for example, writing skills.

PRESUPPOSITIONS OF NLP

One great place to start in exploring new technology is to look at its underlying assumptions, or presuppositions. In NLP, these are useful ways of thinking about people, their problems, communication, needs and values. It is not necessary that you agree with all of these, they are simply the ones we believe allow us to be effective. They are also guidelines for being a persuasive communicator in any medium, not just writing. We invite you to act as if they are true, and see the result.

1. The map is **not** the territory.

This is a very old way of saying that our beliefs and ideas about how people, life and the world work aren't necessarily accurate. They are just a guide, or map, of how things work. It may be that you have been following some old rules or guides about writing that are actually getting in your way, rather than helping you. Maybe it's time for a new map. You're about to get one.

2. All behavior has some "positive" intention. People make the best choices they perceive are available to them.

No matter how weird you think people's or your own behavior is, there is some good reason behind it. Sometimes you have to do a great deal of questioning and thinking to get it to make sense, but with patience and perseverance, you can do it. Maybe you get stuck at certain times in your writing and don't yet know why. Or perhaps you believe that the person you are writing to is evil and dangerous and doesn't deserve to read your brilliant prose. In both cases you can make your task very difficult and even quite painful. If you assume that you have a good reason for being stuck, and that the other person has a good reason for being other than you wish, then that assumption of positive intent can change your thinking—enough to get you going in the direction you need. We'll show you lots of ways later.

3. The meaning of any communication is the response it elicits, regardless of the communicator's intent.

It is really easy to blame others for misinterpreting what you want them to do. Good communicators, especially good writers, take responsibility for getting others to understand them. People respond to what they think they hear, see, or understand. Assume that people are responding appropriately, then figure out how you got them to do it. It will make you think and communicate differently, and understand people much better.

4. The mind/body relationship is cybernetic: a change in one part of the system will affect other parts.

Most people realize that our thinking affects us physically, even to the point of making us sick or well. By the same token, if we are not healthy, or even comfortable, we won't think very well. Learn to control your physical and mental processes effectively, and there is little you can't do.

5. There are no mistakes, only outcomes. There are no failures, only feedback.

Every thing we do, successful or not, can be learned from. If we take results as feedback, they can teach us a lot about how to behave and live. People who kick themselves for their mistakes usually don't take the time to carefully analyze the causes and effects. They don't learn all they can. Those who don't learn from their own history are condemned to repeat it.

6. All of us have all of the internal resources we really need—which doesn't mean we couldn't use a little help in finding them.

People are resilient. They are smart. They are capable. When they don't seem to be any of these things it is because they are not in touch with their internal resources and strengths. The best help is that which gets people to use their own strengths, talents, and gifts. That's why this book is filled with exercises.

7. All the information you need can be obtained through clear and open sensory channels.

We all know that we often look around wildly, and needlessly, for that which is often right in front of us. Whether this is our car keys, the pencil we just put down, the right person for the job, or a new idea, if we pay attention, we will find it. If we don't, we won't.

8. An effective person (writer) needs three characteristics:
   i.   Flexibility of behavior to get results.
   ii. The sensory acuity to notice the results.
   iii. The good judgement to know whether the results are worth getting.

Many problems are created by doing the same things, over and over, whether they work or not. The old saying, "If at first you don't succeed, try, try again" needs to have more added to it. Perhaps, "try, try again, in a new and different way." Flexibility. Also, especially when trying something new, you have to pay close attention to see the results, whether you're working with people or things. Finally, you need to keep in mind that simply being able to get something done doesn't automatically make it a good idea. It needs to be considered in relationship to all the other things that it can effect. This need for awareness is certainly the case in writing.

Corollary—Resistance is a sign that:
   i. Rapport has not been effectively established or maintained.
   ii. Objections have not been properly considered and addressed..

People often complain that others don't, or won't, go along with their ideas. These two corollaries explain why. You have to establish rapport, usually just to get people to pay attention to your ideas. Then you can broach the task of getting them to agree to your ideas or carry them out. Also, you have to be willing to listen to, respect, and respond to the concerns of other people you are involved with. The best, most persuasive, writing in the world won't overcome poor rapport or legitimate objections.

9. The law of requisite variety: The part of any system with the most options in its behavior will be the part that is in control of the system.

Flexibility = options = control. Simple.

10. There is no such thing as a dangerous or unethical process or technique, only dangerous and unethical users (people). It is up to us to know the difference and act accordingly.

Influencing others is neither good nor bad. You must decide that what you're doing has a purpose that is worthwhile. If your intentions include a good and worthwhile outcome for everyone involved, it would be silly, and could even be harmful, not to use your abilities to influence others.

11. If it is possible for someone in the world, it is possible for others. It is only a question of how.

If you believe you are very limited in your abilities, you will act as if those limitations are real. They're not. Act as if you can do anything others can do, and it will motivate you to find out how they do what they do. Then you can do it, too. The procedures we'll show you are based on what effective people do. They work for them, and they'll work for you.

NEURO-LOGICAL LEVELS

The latest, and one of the most useful, contributions NLP has made is called the Neuro-Logical Levels. These are levels of analysis, useful in organizing your thinking, arranged in a hierarchy. This kind of analytic tool has been applied to a number of fields of study and problems to be solved. For our purposes, it can be an extremely helpful "jumping-off point" to check our logic in approaching a writing situation or task. The levels look like this:

Figure 1.1

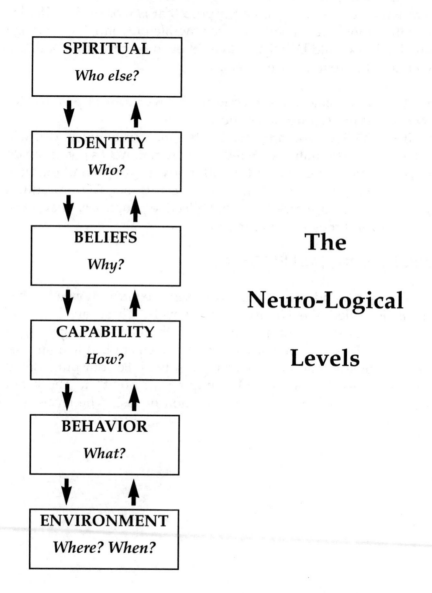

Let's take a good look at this arrangement from the bottom up, because it will make more sense that way. As almost everyone intuitively realizes, a safe and properly designed environment is essential to most projects. For life itself, food, shelter, and security are essential. Writing is certainly no exception, and like other specialized tasks, writing has its own environmental requirements. Most people need a quiet, reasonably comfortable, well-lighted place to gather their thoughts. Also, the right tools are important: things like writing utensils or computer, dictionary and other references, and the other obvious things we've all found we need.

It is also important to consider the time as well as the place. It may be easier and more productive to take on a task if other things are taken care of first, or if interruptions are anticipated.

Though some of these considerations may seem ridiculously obvious, we feel it's still important to be clear about them at the beginning. We are continually astonished at how what is obvious to some people can seem so obscure to others (including us). This is a part of human nature that NLP tries to address in as many ways as possible. As you can see from the above chart, the environmental level is the "where and when" of your writing.

Next we have the behavioral level. This includes thoughts and feelings, as well as all the other activities associated with doing something, in our case writing. For example, many people get quite nervous when it is time to write, even though they are otherwise well prepared. The nervousness is a behavior, and one that will cancel out the value of a whole lot of other behaviors, no matter how efficiently they would otherwise be performed. In addition to controlling thoughts and feelings, there are the many small tasks involved in writing, from deciding what to do at the beginning, to organizing, and creating a finished product. This is the "what" to do when writing, and a great deal of this book will be spent on this, the behavioral level of analysis.

Next we come to the level of capability, the "how" in any task. Obviously it is possible to have the environment arranged perfectly, and to know exactly what has to be done to accomplish the task, but to have no earthly idea how to do it. "How" means capability, processes, procedures, strategies. We find that most educated people know where, when and even what has to be done, when it comes to writing—but they have never really been taught how. Most of the focus of this book, and the NLP techniques we'll teach you, are about how to control the behaviors that make up writing, mentally, emotionally, and organizationally.

No matter how much you know, and how capable you are, you may still not believe in your abilities, or value their worth. If this is the case, you won't use your abilities, even if you can. This is the logical level of beliefs and values, or "why" you should or could do anything. Perhaps you're one of the many people who lost confidence in yourself when you were learning to write in school. Maybe you had help in this from the school, your peers, your family, or some other well-intentioned but ultimately defeating outside force. Now maybe you've "internalized" this defeated attitude so you no longer try. If this is the case, you're in luck. It turns out that most of the people who have come out of school with shattered self-confidence can rebuild their belief in themselves with just a little practice. The advantage you'll have going through the procedures we'll give you is that they will simultaneously build back your self-esteem as they build in success in writing. The message you'll get, loud and clear, is that it isn't your fault you've had a hard time writing. It never was your fault. It was simply the result of poor technology in teaching youngsters to write efficiently and effectively, and to enjoy it as well.

The sum of your behaviors, your capabilities and your beliefs is your identity, "who" you are, in anything that you do. Built in to our writing model is the notion of choosing an appropriate role for each writing project. But beyond that, your identity as a unique individual is something that can never be taken away from you. It can be the source of your strength and value as a writer as well. No one else has been created exactly like you. Without a firm sense of your identity, however, you can easily founder. We'll ask you, often, to make sure you are congruent, consistent within yourself, while you take on a writing task. This sense of your own specialness can be important for everything else in your life, too.

Finally, we have the spiritual level of analysis, which examines how you are connected to the world outside of yourself. The spiritual level does not necessarily have anything to do with religion, but it could. Essentially, it means "who else" besides you is involved with you, your identity, your beliefs, capabilities, and behaviors. In writing, this sense of interconnectedness is especially important, as it is in all communication. None of us operates in a vacuum. We are connected to others somehow, and if we remain aware of that connection, and use it in effective ways, we'll certainly be much better writers. Probably better people, also.

Chapter Two

The Context Of POWER

Communication doesn't happen by itself, in a vacuum. There is always a context. That is, somebody wants to get a message to somebody else by some means in some kind of circumstance. And communication isn't really a thing; it's a process. That is, somebody has to send the message, and somebody has to receive it. One familiar model looks like this:

Figure 2.1
Basic Communication Model

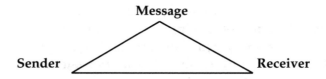

THE COMMUNICATION PROCESS

Communicating isn't as simple as the diagram makes it seem, though. Let's take a closer look at the process, considering some of the possible problem points. Messages can be sent in many ways, of course—words (spoken or written), music, movement (dancing, fighting, unintentional body language), sculpture, etc. Since this book is about writing, however, we'll concentrate on that.

The Writer's Part

To get very far into the writing process, a writer must first be inspired by an idea. That a writer needs an idea may seem obvious to you now, but many writers have been stuck because they really didn't have anything to say. This situation is all too common in school, with assigned topics. Many people have gotten the notion that they "couldn't write" because they couldn't produce essays about topics they found to be irrelevant.

Suppose the idea is there, though. We began this book with clear ideas about writing—how to make it easier, more comfortable, more effective, efficient, and fun. Next, after the idea, a writer needs some basic tools—pencil and paper, word processor, or some other tool. Well, yes, how simple. But haven't you ever lost an idea because you couldn't find a pencil—and had forgotten why you wanted it by the time you found it? Dixie loses more good poetry lines that way. They come while she's out walking, and by the time she's arrived home.... Or maybe you've put off writing because it would be easier once you got to your own familiar computer? Dixie's guilty there, too. She hates to think about having to re-type things.

Assuming the idea and tools are there, next the writer has to encode it—to put the idea into words. And yes, obstacles to the process may arise here, too. Ideas aren't always born in words; sometimes we get pictures in our heads, or feelings we want to express. Probably everyone has experienced the frustration of impoverished code—of having a great idea but no words to express it. That's one of Sid's bugaboos. He gets great pictures in his head, but he can't draw, so he has to translate his pictures into words.

Interference can come from outside the process itself, too. Sid can't write until he's washed all the dishes. That's only true for his own dishes, however; he's never compelled to clean Dixie's kitchen. Once started, though, suppose the writer is happily putting wonderful words on paper, and the phone rings. Or the power goes out. Or it becomes time for another appointment of some sort. Or bedtime. Life, including other people, goes on and seldom agrees to wait until we finish the next sentence. Fortunately, good writers have strategies to take them right back to where they were in the process when they were interrupted. Interruptions may delay things, but they don't have to disrupt the writing process. We'll show you how to do it, too, so your *interruptions* will no longer be *disruptions*.

The Message Alone

Even if the writer completes the writing, communication hasn't happened yet. Only the first stage of the process has been completed. The message still has to get to the reader and be decoded. Between mail service and filing systems on people's desks, many misadventures are possible for the message. In the case of this book, before it got to you, we had to sell it to a publisher, who in turn had to package and market it so that you could select it in the store or catalog.

The Reader's Part

Let's suppose that the message has indeed made it to the final stage of the process. It is in the hands of the intended reader, who is eager to decode it—to take the words and turn them into the idea the writer intended to convey. For example, when you bought this book, how did you picture yourself using it? What did you tell yourself? What memories about writing came up that prompted you to look at it? Then how did you become sure this book would solve your writing problems? And how has that scenario progressed so far?

As a reader, you are subject to the same kinds of interferences as the writer was. Your phone rings, too. Fatigue sets in. Or your big labrador retriever bounds in to play, pretends the book is supper, and....

Subject matter itself can be an interference for some people. Writing is a prime example. Some people have such negative feelings about writing that they can hardly bear to think about it, much less read a book about it. Since one of our main objectives is to make writing more comfortable for you, we're especially conscious of that one.

Once you actually start decoding—reading—the message, language may again be a problem. What if we've used unfamiliar words? Is there a dictionary handy? Would you stop reading to look up a word you were unsure of? Really?

A more insidious problem occurs when the writer uses a word to mean something different from the meaning the reader thinks of first. Dixie recalls a down-home example. She had a new baby-sitter for her fourteen-month-old child and called home to check on things. The sitter was reassuring—they'd had lunch, Kyla was napping, and then, "She's starting to wake up now. Oh, oh, she's ill. Let me go." Click. With visions of her child sick and crying,

Dixie hurriedly closed down her office and raced home. Kyla and the sitter were cheerfully coloring. No sign of distress. Questioned, the sitter said, "Oh, no she's fine. She was just whiny, a little cranky, you know." Yes, ill-*tempered*. Dixie got the message all right, but not the right message. The picture in her head didn't match the picture the sitter had intended to convey.

Communicating In Context

Taking into account the complexity of influences in the writing process, a more realistic model of the communication process might look like this:

Figure 2.2
The Communication Process

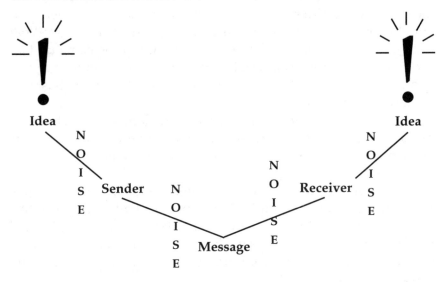

It may seem that in the normal course of everyday life, so many things can interfere with communication that our ever understanding each other is a miracle. Well, yes, it is, rather. Fortunately, we believe in miracles. One miracle is that an awareness of the complexity of human communication is a strong tool for making our communication effective. Communication always happens in a context.

Trying to communicate without considering the context is like trying to communicate in a vacuum. Do you remember how much life exits in a vacuum? Right—none! When we try to write in a vacuum—without an awareness of the context of our communication—not much happens. That's why we place our model of the writing process in the total context of communication, and we begin each writing project with previewing: getting a look at the specific context for this writing task.

THE *POWER* MODEL OF THE WRITING PROCESS

Many people have tried to define the process of writing. One of the most popular models has three steps: prewriting, writing, and rewriting. Another has nine steps. We could probably create a new model of the writing process for each writer, each one slightly different; there is no ONE WAY that must be followed. Yet there are certain basic patterns every successful writer follows.

The model we use has five major steps, with one of them subdivided. It paces the process, in general terms, used by every successful writer we know. The five steps are Previewing, Organizing, Writing, Evaluating, and Revising; we call it the POWER model.

Previewing

The first step in the writing process is *previewing*. In this stage you look over the writing situation—your communication context—before getting bogged down. The better the job done in this stage, the less time is spent later, undoing or redoing what you've written. Because this stage is so important, we've subdivided it into five components: self, purpose, audience, code, and experience—SPACE.

Self is a good place to begin. Who are you, the writer? We all wear many hats, and we choose which of the many facets of our personality we will display in any given situation. Your personal identity—who you are at your core and in your soul—is complex and too vast to find complete expression in any one given context. Your role is that part of you that needs expression in this situation. Begin by clearly defining for yourself the role you're playing in this context, the image of yourself you want to project.

Purpose is the next consideration. Why are you writing? When the writing is done, and when the reader has finished it, what do you want to happen? Sometimes we have more than one purpose; there may be one overt purpose and one or more secondary ones. Understanding your own motivations improves your chances of getting what you want.

Audience (more fully—*audience analysis*) is obviously a critical factor, yet it is the one element most frequently overlooked. Since writing is essentially a solitary task, it's easy to lose sight of the context of the communication itself, especially of that person on the other end of the process. Yet audience awareness (hence analysis) should have a strong impact on your writing.

Code is your next consideration. Code refers to the means by which you present your message. In the writing process, we use words; you must decide what level of language to use. Format is also a consideration of code. Are you going to write a memo or a letter, a formal report or a list? You may even decide a phone call would be more appropriate than writing.

Experience is the last element in the previewing stage. What personal experience do you have with the content of your message? Do you have enough information in your head or in books or files at hand, or do you need to gather more information, perhaps by making a phone call to an expert or by doing library research?

You've probably realized that these previewing components are all interrelated, as illustrated by the diagram below. Your experience is dependent on your role, which is influenced by your purpose, which is connected to your audience, who will determine your language code. All these factors will affect the amount and kind of detail or experience you use.

Figure 2.3
POWER *Previewing* SPACE

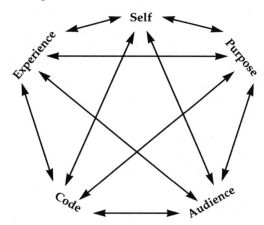

Working through these elements translates into ease of writing in the rest of the process. Later, we'll help you do it systematically to start you on your way to becoming a POWERful writer.

Organizing

Getting your information organized is the second step in the writing process. Given your audience and purpose, what arrangement of your material will be most effective? If the previewing process hasn't made organizing seem almost automatic (it often does), we have some tools that will help.

Writing

We call the middle stage of the process *writing*, although you may very well have done some writing in the first two steps. In this writing stage, you produce your first draft. The object of writing the first draft is to get all the information you want to include out of your head, note cards, or files and onto paper. You want to collect your thoughts in one place, externally, so that you can see the message independently from yourself (the message sender).

Evaluating

Once you have a draft of your message, you can look at it objectively and evaluate it. Does it say what you meant? Will your audience read it the way you intended? Will it accomplish your purpose? Could you make it more effective?

Revising

Evaluating your writing will usually lead you to the final step. Revising means seeing again, and then you rewrite to reach your new vision. Finally, you look at the surface of the writing, correcting any errors that might distract a reader from your message. Although grammatical sophisticates maintain an unfocused awareness of such things automatically, you'll want to save deliberate proofing for spelling, punctuation, or grammar slips for *the very last act* in the writing process.

All of this may seem quite complicated—and it is. But like most other complex tasks in life, with a little practice and organization, it can become simple and automatic.

POWER DYNAMICS

As you think about your own writing process, you'll probably recognize these steps. Of course, the process can be drawn out or contracted, depending on the length and complexity of the writing task. For instance, for a brief thank you note to your Aunt Minnie, you will probably preview, organize, draft, and evaluate in your head; your first actual physical writing will come at the revising step. On the other hand, a formal application for a grant will probably go through several drafts and multiple evaluations.

We present this model in a linear fashion, as if writers move sequentially from previewing, to organizing, to writing, to evaluating and to revising. Overall, we do. But as you further compare this model and your own writing process, you may become aware of some looping movement, some recursion and repetition. The important thing to remember is that writing is a *process* involving both physical and mental activity. This book will guide you through the process, step by step, concentrating on how to make the process work for you. As you look at the model, you'll see the acronym POWER SPACE. Writing is indeed a tool of power, and we'll show you how to develop your own writing power. As you follow our suggestions throughout the writing process, you'll begin to regard a blank piece of paper not as something intimidating, but as the **power space** for your ideas.

Chapter Three

The POWER Of
Neuro-Linguistic Programming

Having an understanding of the writing process is one thing. Actually getting into the process comfortably and effectively, is, for many people, quite another. This chapter will introduce you to the techniques we can use to get ourselves in gear, to motivate ourselves to really do what we intend to do. You'll learn how you can tap your own powers of concentration and your best internal resources to accomplish the things you want to do.

INTRODUCTION TO NLP

"Neuro WHAT?" is the usual response when we say "Neuro-Linguistic Programming" to the uninitiated. That is one of the reasons it has that name: it fosters curiosity. "Neuro" pays tribute to the brain, that marvelous organ that controls so much. "Linguistic" acknowledges the power of language on the way we think. "Programming" puts the emphasis on the way we direct our brains to function. Once the confusion about the name passes, people find one of the most fascinating sets of tools they have ever experienced. Although NLP will soon be familiar to all literate people, we recognize that it is presently unknown to most. Out of the many books and articles available on NLP, we've included some of our favorites in the bibliography.

Of course you don't need all the techniques and models of NLP to be an effective writer. But some of them can help tremendously. We're going to introduce you to NLP techniques for motivation, creativity, decision making, objectivity, and other universally useful components. Then we'll show you how to use them to make yourself a more effective writer.

Like any specialized field, NLP has its own jargon—shorthand names for labeling certain sets of experience. Here are some of the most important:

States Of Consciousness

State of mind, state of awareness, mood, etc. are all roughly synonymous with states of consciousness. From now on, we'll simply call them states. For our purposes, we are interested in particular states—for example, the right state of mind for writing, for getting organized, or for being creative. The important thing is that we learn a method for distinguishing one state from another, so that we can explore its usefulness, modify it as we see fit, control it, and get it whenever we want.

Actually, we all go in and out of many states of consciousness all the time. Probably hundreds each day. These are what are called natural states, though this probably isn't the most useful term. Neither is the term "altered state," since that almost makes them sound unnatural. Some states are easier to tell from others, however, just in our own experience of them. So it is usually best to talk about that experience of being in a particular state as compared to some other. That's what we'll be concentrating on here.

This brings us to the method for identifying particular discrete states. The elements that help us define a given state of consciousness are based on the five senses: visual (sight), auditory (hearing), kinesthetic (feelings), olfactory (smell), and gustatory (taste). In a particular state of mind, external sensory detail is less important than our internal experience. In our system, visual refers to our internal pictures, auditory to our internal sounds, kinesthetic to feelings (both tactile and internal), and olfactory-gustatory (combined for convenience) to smells and tastes. A particular state is simply the sum total of each of these four components at a given time. Remember, this is only an experiential definition of a state. It doesn't include any objectively verifiable physiological data (blood pressure, metabolic rate, temperature, respiration, EEG readings, galvanic skin response, etc.) because that isn't important for our purpose. Be aware that these things do change along with our experiences, but measuring them is irrelevant in this context.

Changing one part of a given state has a ripple effect on the other parts. That is how we go from one state of mind to another. We can control our internal images, the voices in our heads and so forth, so we can choose at will to change the states we don't like to ones we do. To begin with, we can think of each of the sensory modes as an independent part. For example, often we are aware of our internal visualizations (literally, the pictures in our minds) to the exclusion of all else. The same can be said of our feelings, our internal voices, and so on. Changing our awareness from one sense to another, therefore, can alter our total experience. When we talk about expanding (heightening, increasing, etc.) our awareness, that is a major part of what we really mean.

Certainly we can change the *content* of our internal images to change our feelings and overall experience of some event. A common exercise given to performers to overcome stage fright is to imagine the audience in some compromising position, like sitting in their underwear. It works because it is difficult to be frightened by people who are in a more vulnerable (or even ridiculous) position than we are. Most of us have played games of that sort before in the privacy of our own thoughts. But few of us do so systematically, whenever it would help us to be more at ease or effective. We could.

Becoming aware of the sensory modes themselves, and their influences on our states of mind, is a first step toward our main purpose, which is to be able to get ourselves into good states (useful, productive) and to stay out of bad ones (stuck, unproductive). After all, what are states made of but sensory experience? You've probably heard it in the language people use as they try to represent their experience: "I can see the light at the end of the tunnel"; "I'm really tuned in"; "I wanted it so badly I could taste it." What we say often reflects the sensory modality (also called a representational system) that is most strongly influential in our experience: visual—"see the light;" auditory—"tuned in;" or olfactory-gustatory—"taste it," for example.

Sub-Modalities

So, a full sensory experience is built up from smaller components, the modalities of vision, hearing, etc. Each sensory modality is made up of even smaller components called sub-modalitites. Besides changing the content of our internal thoughts, we can change our experience by changing the sub-modalities of a part of the state. Within each sensory mode, there are a number of characteristics that make up the form of the content within that mode. For example, one of the sub-modalities of the visual mode (i.e., internal pictures) is brightness. Another is size. Another is color. Each of these can be changed without making a new image, but the *form* or *quality* of the image will certainly be different. And this difference will also register itself in some other part of our experience—like our feelings.

We are talking, then, about a smaller chunk of experience than each individual sensory mode. The sub-modality level is, in a way, the most basic (though not the most important or best) level on which to control your state of consciousness. A simple change at the sub-modality level can instantly change every other level of experience simultaneously and, sometimes, *permanently*. We'll come back to the sub-modalities soon. For the moment, take a look at the following diagram to help put these relationships in perspective.

Figure 3.1
The Structure Of Sensory Experience And State

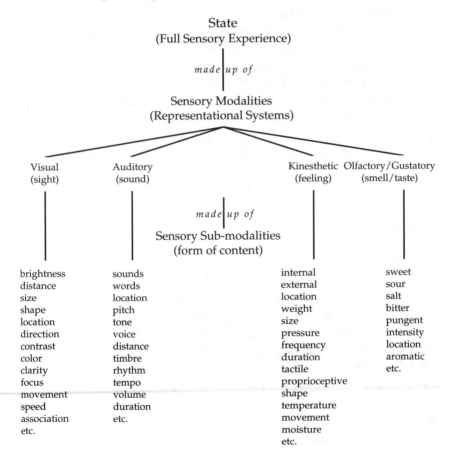

State
(Full Sensory Experience)

made up of

Sensory Modalities
(Representational Systems)

Visual (sight)	Auditory (sound)		Kinesthetic (feeling)	Olfactory/Gustatory (smell/taste)
		made up of Sensory Sub-modalities (form of content)		
brightness	sounds		internal	sweet
distance	words		external	sour
size	location		location	salt
shape	pitch		weight	bitter
location	tone		size	pungent
direction	voice		pressure	intensity
contrast	distance		frequency	location
color	timbre		duration	aromatic
clarity	rhythm		tactile	etc.
focus	tempo		proprioceptive	
movement	volume		shape	
speed	duration		temperature	
association	etc.		movement	
etc.			moisture	
			etc.	

Anchoring

How do we get back a particular state that we want? Well, for a moment, think about your memory. When you recall some event or experience you have had, how do you actually remember it? What causes the images and sounds in your head to come flooding back to you? What is the mechanism that causes you to react to something with a response, whether the response is an act, thought, or feeling?

We have all had the experience of going about our normal routine, minding our own business, and suddenly being struck by a memory. Often, if we pay attention to our surroundings, we can identify some object, sound, or smell that seems to be the cause of our sudden recall. It could be anything. A stranger's facial expression or posture can remind us of someone we know. We then have a memory that involved that person, and suddenly we have a set of images, sounds, and feelings that go with that memory. It is as if we are not in our present surroundings any longer but have been hurled back in time to that former place. We are with that person again in our own minds, and we have the experiences that go along with that former place and time. Sound familiar? Of course.

The memories and the specific things that trigger them are unique to each individual, but the process by which the triggering mechanism works is universal. That particular facial expression, song, or scent may affect only you, or it may affect you in ways very different from the person next to you. And certainly the memory you have is all yours. But we are *all* affected by *some* facial expression, song, or scent at some time. That is a universal experience.

In NLP we call this process *anchoring*. This basic sort of cause-effect relationship when two sets of experiences become associated can be observed in just about all animals, even one-celled bacteria. Pavlov used it in his famous conditioning experiments. Here's a comparison of anchoring and conditioning:

Figure 3.2
Comparison Of Pavlovian Conditioning And NLP Anchoring

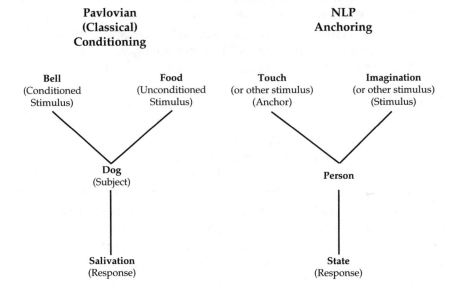

The process is roughly the same, but in human beings, the results can be much more dramatic. Moreover, we have an advantage in that we can simply use our imaginations to present ourselves with a stimulus. You can test that idea quickly by vividly imagining biting into a juicy lemon.

In other words, as human beings we have the intellectual capacity to control the stimuli that we're exposed to by creating them with our thoughts and memories. This is the mechanism we can use to control our states of mind. Pick the right memory, and get the right state. This is power.

So Neuro-Linguistic Programming is the study of how these mental processes actually work—and how we can use them to our best advantage. For the rest of this book, we'll be giving you explicit instructions for using these naturally occurring processes yourself. Remember also, that even though we are focusing our attention on making you a better and more efficient writer, these ideas and techniques can be used for just about anything. You are limited only by your own imagination.

EXPERIENCING NEURO-LINGUISTIC PROGRAMMING

The easiest way to understand anchoring, and these other terms and processes—what they are and how they work—is through experience. We'll experiment with a state of mind very useful in writing: excitement and enthusiasm. Suppose someone asked you to remember a time when you were especially enthusiastic and excited. How would you do it? You'd probably do some sort of backward search through your memory for an experience that you have "filed away" in the "excitement and enthusiasm" drawer. More specifically, would you sort through a series of internal visual images until you had a feeling of excitement? Would these images look, literally, like a series of snapshots? Would it look more like a movie? Or would you perhaps simply say the word "excitement" to yourself, and then feel it? Some people seem able to adjust their feelings at will and then find a past visual image that "fits" the feeling. Take a moment now to find out how you would do it.

Setting An Anchor For A State Of Consciousness

You have already taken the first step to anchor your own excitement. Now, we'll make the rest of the process more explicit.

Establishing The State Of Excitement

1. Remember that time when you were very excited and enthusiastic, vividly and completely.

2. When you have the feeling of excitement, pay attention to the visual images in your mind. Avoid making judgments about them; just notice what they are.

3. When you have a clear picture firmly held in your mind, notice the set of physical sensations that go with it. What, exactly, does this state of excitement feel like, physically, for you?

4. Next pay attention to any internal sounds you have in your mind. You may be talking to yourself; most of us do that much of the time. If so, notice what you are saying and how the voice sounds. Are there other sounds as well, music, perhaps, or other voices?

5.   Notice now the last components—smell and taste. Do you notice any? As you pay attention to each of your senses, be aware that you are discovering exactly what, for you, constitutes this state of excitement. Realize also that this state was a response to whatever you did in your head to create it.

6.   When you know what you did to get the state of excitement (what pictures you saw, sounds you heard, feelings you felt, smells and tastes you experienced), get up and walk around for a moment to distract yourself.

7.   Sit back down and go back into that state of excitement again. As you do so, find out if you immediately go from your "normal" state to your state of excitement. Many people do. If you don't, go back through the steps you went through before and see which of the last few seem necessary to get you into this state. If you've ever done it before (even if you haven't actually done it, but you can imagine how it would be), you can do it again. The point here is to find your naturally occurring method of getting to the state of excitement and enthusiasm.

This basic experiment helps you focus on what you do in your mind. It will also help you determine what stimulates you to this feeling, or state, of excitement and enthusiasm. For example, perhaps you went through a sequence of steps to get into the state. Maybe you first thought of the word "excitement," then made an image of some time when you felt that way, then imagined yourself back in that other time and voila! Excitement! It may be that doing any of those steps is all you need to get back that feeling. It could also simply be that the last step you did inside your head before the excitement hit you was the crucial one. Often that last step is the trigger. Finding what the internal trigger for the state is can be a very valuable learning experience, because no matter how you did it, you did it yourself, under your own control.

In NLP we call that trigger, or stimulus, an anchor. An anchor can be almost anything, as long as it works. For some people it will be a visual image; for others, a sound, or another feeling. Some people even get a particular taste in their mouths or a smell just prior to the response. The important thing is to discover what is a working, already naturally occurring anchor for this state. You may even have several.

When you have determined your anchor for excitement, practice it a few times. Often, an anchor becomes stronger with use, especially when there is some payoff for it. Excitement might be a most useful tool for you when you write. Practice, use, and remember this anchor. We'll come back to it later.

Enhancing A State Of Consciousness

A good thing can often be made better, so let's explore using the sub-modalities to enhance your state of enthusiasm and excitement. Think, for a moment, about television. Nearly all of us have used one at some time in our lives. As the technology has improved over the years, we have had more and more control over the picture and sound quality of our sets. Now some of them have stereo, huge screens, remarkable resolution and color, cable hookups to make the picture and sound crystal clear, video cassette recorders or disc players, and more. All these enhancements change our overall experience of watching and listening to television. Have you ever wondered what it would be like to exercise those same kinds of control over the pictures in our minds? That's exactly what the sub-modalities are for.

For this exercise, as an option, you may wish to read the instructions into a tape recorder. Then you can play back the instructions to yourself so you can do the exercise without being distracted by looking back at this book to see what's next. Or you may wish to enlist a friend as coach for this part. The whole process of exploring how changes in your sub-modalities affect your state of consciousness may take from twenty to forty minutes.

Visual Sub-Modalities

Enhancing Your State Of Excitement: Visual Adjustments

1.   Remember the visual image attached to your feeling of excitement and enthusiasm. (You may use another feeling, if you like; just be sure it's a nice feeling.)

2.   Imagine putting the scene on hold, if it is moving, so that it looks like a still shot or a slide rather than a motion picture. Hold it steady in your mind's eye. Notice the quality of the picture, the size, color, brightness, whether it has a frame around it, and anything unusual that strikes you.

3.   Pay close attention to the feeling you have in your body that you label excitement and enthusiasm (or whatever the feeling is that you've chosen). Notice especially how intense the feeling is.

4.   Now imagine that you have a brightness control knob next to the image in your mind's eye, just like the one on a television set. Imagine turning up the brightness, slowly, and watch the image in your mind get brighter, just as it would if it were on your television screen. Make the image noticeably brighter, but still clearly the same image. Don't let it get so bright that it begins to get hazy or break up.

5.   Now pay attention to the feeling that goes along with that internal image. Has it changed in any way? How?

6.   Try steps 1-5 again, this time with images associated with different (but still pleasant) feelings. Notice what changes occur in your feelings, especially the intensity of them, each time you turn up the brightness of your pictures.

Variation 1: Return to your original image, the picture for excitement and enthusiasm, and repeat steps 1-3. At step 4, instead of turning the brightness up, turn it down. Again, make the dimness noticeable, but don't let it get so dim that you can't recognize the picture. Now pay attention to the feelings and how they have changed. Again notice the intensity. Do the same with the other images you brightened earlier. Be sure to adjust them to the way you like them best before you stop.

Variation 2: Repeat the exercise, but this time, change the size of the image rather than the brightness. Imagine it has gone from its original size to a giant screen size. Try the exercise again, making the picture smaller instead of larger, from its original size to a tiny pocket-size screen. How do the changes in size affect your feelings as compared to the changes in brightness?

Variation 3: Do the exercise once more, this time with color. First make the colors extremely distinct—more vivid than the original. Then try the reverse. Change the color all the way to black and white, or even shades of gray. Compare the changes in your feelings to the changes you got from adjusting size and brightness.

You may have been surprised by the effects on your feelings of simply altering one aspect, or sub-modality, of the image. Although most people aren't consciously aware of this influence, you've probably heard people talk about it. Do you know someone, for example, who's led a colorful life? Who remembers back in the dim and distant past? Who's looking forward to a bright future? By contrast, have you ever heard people say they remembered their bright distant past? Or that they were looking forward to a dim future? Or that something was a very small and powerful experience in their lives? Probably not. Those odd-sounding phrases don't make much sense because they don't match the way our minds process information. Our language, in many ways, is a very direct reflection of our internal, often unconscious, experience. Sometimes listening closely to language can give us some conscious insight into the underlying thought processes.

You've explored varying three of the visual sub-modalities. There are other possibilities. Here is an outline of the major visual sub-modalities, followed by a brief explanation of each.

Visual Sub-Modalities

Color	Shape	Size	Distance
Location	Frame/No frame	Brightness	Contrast
Clarity	Focus	Movement/Speed	Direction
Depth (3-D/flat)	Slide/Motion Picture	Associated/Disassociated	

Color. Color means the one(s) you see. Is the picture black and white, full color, or a combination? Does one color stand out as central or important somehow?

Shape, Size, Distance, Location, And Frame. Shape means the shape of the image itself, as well as any internal shapes that stand out in the picture. The same goes for size, distance, and location. For example, your image may be a 2' X 3' rectangle, about six feet away, directly in front of you. It may appear to have a frame, or some sort of border around it. It may, by contrast, be panoramic, completely surrounding you in it.

Brightness, Contrast, Clarity And Focus. Brightness and contrast mean the same as they would in adjusting the picture on a television set. How bright is the picture? How sharp is the contrast of elements in the image? Clarity and focus are similar. How clearly do you see details in the image?

Slides/Motion Picture And Depth. Whether you see an internal image as a still shot, like a slide or photograph, or as a motion picture can be crucial. So can the depth perception of the image; it could be flat and two-dimensional like a photo or appear to be a three-dimensional slide or, more dramatically, a hologram.

Movement/Speed And Direction. If you have a motion picture, the speed and direction of motion could be important. For example, the motion may be exactly as it would be in "real life," or it could be in slow motion. The movement could be in chronological sequence, or it could be going backwards (a useful way to remember unpleasant events).

Associated/Disassociated. An associated image is one in which you see exactly what you would see, through your own eyes as if you were there. In other words, you would not see yourself in the image, just as you do not see your whole self now.

A disassociated image is just the opposite. You see yourself in the picture, as if you were looking through someone else's eyes. Imagine for a moment that you are in a room with a group of people and you are being videotaped. What you see while you are in the room is an associated image. The playback that you see later from the tape is disassociated, since you see yourself from another point of view, that of the camera. When people talk about needing a different point of view or a change in perspective, often they are talking about, quite literally, changing from associated to disassociated images in their minds.

In NLP we often discuss the value of exploring different perceptual positions. We distinguish between first, second, and third position (much as in English class, first person, second person, third person: I, you, they). First position is associated. You experience the image from your original position, looking out through your own eyes. Second position would be imagining that you were another person in the experience you were remembering. If you were remembering a conversation with another person, for example, remembering it as it actually happened to you would be first position for you—possibly fully panoramic as well. Second position would be literally remembering it (actually imagining it) from the other person's viewpoint. In second position, you imagine you are looking out through the eyes of that other person, with all their thoughts and perceptions. Third position, by contrast, is taking the viewpoint of "the fly on the wall." In this case, you would imagine you could see both yourself and the other person clearly, from an outside perspective. You would have your own perceptions, but since you were, in a sense, separate from yourself in the image, your feelings would be altered. Here's a diagram of the three perceptual positions:

Figure 3.3
Three Perceptual Positions

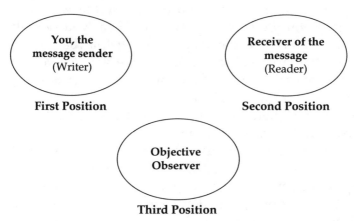

Auditory Sub-Modalities

We began with visual sub-modalities because they are easiest for most people at first. Internal auditory (sound) changes can be just as dramatic. You simply need to find which changes will work to affect you in the way you want.

Enhancing A State Of Consciousness: Auditory Adjustments

1.   Remember the sound of a particular person's voice. This time, make it some voice that intimidated you when you last heard it. The situation doesn't matter, or whether you like or dislike the person. What is important is that you felt some amount of fear or anxiety when you heard that voice and you still do now as you hear it in your mind. For some people, it helps to remember the particular visual image that went along with the situation and then become aware of the voice.

2.   Make sure that you can clearly hear the voice inside your head. Pay special attention to the quality of the voice, as well as the words being spoken. Is the voice high or low, loud or soft, in front of you or to the side, raspy or clear? Make sure you know what it sounds like in your mind.

3.   When you have a clear idea of what the voice sounds like, pay close attention to your feelings. Make sure the feelings that go along with this voice are strong and defined.

4.   Now let's find out what happens when you change auditory sub-modalities. Without changing the words, volume, direction, or location, give the voice the tempo and tonal quality of that famous film star, Donald Duck!

5.   Pay attention to the feelings now as you listen to this altered voice. You probably don't feel intimidated anymore, do you?

Variations: If you'd like to explore the impact of auditory sub-modality changes a little more now, repeat the exercise, making different voice changes. You might try moving the voice to a different location or turning the volume of the voice down. Be cautious when you try turning the volume up. Greater volume often intensifies the feelings, so for that variation you might want to choose another voice and situation— one you'll enjoy more than intimidation.

It's difficult to feel intimidated or awed by someone who sounds like a silly cartoon or someone with a soft and distant voice. Even with the voice saying exactly what it said the first time, when you make a change in the quality of the voice, you also change the quality of the experience. You haven't changed the content (words), but you've changed the form (sound quality) and so changed your whole state of consciousness. Altered voice, altered feeling, altered state.

Here is a table of the most important auditory sub-modalities and a brief explanation of each.

Auditory Sub-Modalities

Sound/Words	Internal/External	Voice (Whose?)	Location
Direction	Distance	Volume	Rhythm
Tempo	Duration	Pitch	Tone
Timbre			

Sound/Words. The first distinction to make is whether you hear sounds, words, or both, in your mind. At different times, we can hear a variety of sounds inside our minds, just as we do externally.

Internal/External. Although we're talking about the sounds in your mind, sometimes they seem to be coming from inside your own head, and sometimes they seem to be coming from somewhere on the outside. This becomes especially important when we seem to hear a voice. Even when we imagine a voice, it can still sound as if it is located outside of our heads—as if it is coming from somewhere away from us.

Voice (Whose?). If we hear a voice, a distinction should be made about whose voice it is. We may recognize it as some particular person. Sometimes we won't recognize it, but it may still be clearly male or female, old or young, or some other characteristic. All these qualities will help us recognize, reproduce, or change the sound.

Location, Direction, And Distance. Whether the sound seems inside or outside your head, the location can be important. Then the direction from which the sound is coming as well as the apparent distance may be determined.

Volume. Volume, the loudness or softness of the sound, is often important. It may also be related to distance or location.

Rhythm, Tempo, And Duration. Most sounds have a particular rhythm, or beat, especially if they are musical. Tempo refers to the speed of the sound and/or the rhythm. Duration means how long the sound lasts.

Pitch. Pitch simply means whether the sound is high or low— high notes and/or low notes.

Tone And Timbre. Tone and timbre refer to frequency ranges and distributions. Without getting into the technical details, think of the way two brass instruments sound, say trumpet and saxophone. Even when playing the same note (same pitch), the two instruments sound different. The difference is one of tone and timbre. Voices have the same distinctions. A contralto and a child singing the same note sound very different.

Kinesthetic Sub-Modalities

Changes in our mental pictures or the auditory component of our experience can change how and what we feel, but we can also make adjustments directly to our feelings.

Enhancing A State Of Excitement: Kinesthetic Adjustments

1. Return to your state of excitement and enthusiasm, either your original one or an enhanced one. You may want to use your visual image to help you get there. Or you may find there's an effective auditory element.

2. Pay particular attention to the kinesthetic components of the state. You analyzed those feelings to some extent earlier, but now pay closer attention to the details. Where are you breathing (high chest, lower abdomen), at what speed, and how deeply? Is there some warmth associated with the feeling? How warm, and where is the warmth? What about muscular tension? Notice especially your posture and physical position, whether you are sitting, lying down, or even standing. Are you balanced physically?

3. Change your breathing to a slower tempo and gradually deepen and lower your breath, until you're enjoying long, very slow, full breaths deep from the diaphragm.

4. Pay attention to the changes in your feelings, your emotions. Has the excitement lessened? Has the change in breathing caused other physiological changes, perhaps in the degree or location of muscle tension? Have changes occurred in your visual image?

Variation 1: Try the opposite change in breathing. Make it faster, more shallow, and bring it higher into the chest. Be careful here, though, and stop before you take your excitement into something more like panic.

Variation 2: This time simply change your entire physical position. If you were sitting, or lying down, stand up and move. If you were leaning one way, or slouched, straighten up. What changes does physically moving cause in your feelings and your overall state?

To change your state of consciousness, you only have to change one sub-modality. The key is finding the right sub-modality for you in a given situation. Just as the visual and auditory changes you made can affect your feelings, so also you can change a small part of your feelings and get greater changes in the whole. You have a great many choices. You'll find that when you have determined how a particular sub-modality change affects you, you will have a new tool for changing your experience. That sub-modality change will usually work the same way for you each time you use it. For example, if you find that brightening a particular visual image increases the intensity of the feelings attached to that image, it will undoubtedly work for all your visual images the same way (whether they, and the feelings that go with them, are pleasant or not). Pay close attention and make sure that you create the states you really want.

Here is a list of kinesthetic sub-modalities with a brief explanation of each:

Kinesthetic Sub-Modalities

Internal/External	Tactile/Proprioceptive	Intensity
Location	Shape	Size
Moisture	Weight	Pressure
Temperature	Texture	Duration
Frequency	Movement	Rhythm
Balance		

Internal/External And Tactile/Proprioceptive. One of the first considerations of kinesthetics is whether your feelings are on the inside or the outside. Tactile sensations are those you feel on the outside—your sense of touch. Proprioception means internal feelings, which include muscle tension, the sensations of body position, and so forth.

Intensity. How strong the overall emotion is may be influenced by the intensity, or lack of intensity, of one of the kinesthetic components.

Location, Shape, And Size. Some things (muscle tension, for example) can be felt in very specific areas of our body or on our skin. Some feelings also seem to have size and shape to them. People with writer's block sometimes say, "There's a knot in my stomach about the size of my fist."

Moisture. Moisture is something we can feel on our skin, especially in our palms. Our mouths often feel very wet or dry, especially during certain emotions or around food.

Weight, Pressure, And Temperature. These three qualities may be felt internally or externally. When pressure is felt downward, we generally use weight to indicate intensity of the pressure, but we often refer to pressure building up inside. Lack of pressure may also be equated with weight, as we notice the lightness or a floating sensation. Temperature may vary from inside to out and from various parts of the body.

Texture. Texture is generally limited to external, tactile sensations, although we often ascribe texture to certain emotions (a cold, prickly feeling or a warm, fuzzy one).

Duration And Frequency. Some kinesthetic sensations come and go, so duration (how long) and frequency (how often) may be important.

Movement And Rhythm. Movement and rhythm may be felt both internally and externally and are closely related to duration and frequency. If a movement is repeated, the duration of the movement and the frequency of the repetition create its rhythm. Becoming aware of the rhythm of natural functions like breath and heart rate can be quite powerful.

Balance. Most often balance refers to one's equilibrium or poise. But it may be measured in body symmetry or asymmetry: the similarity or difference of position of the right and left sides of the body.

Feelings have a special place in our behavior, and some of these qualities of feeling seem to be the deciding factors in the overall quality of our experience. Obviously, paying special attention to them can make a great difference in both our experiences and our abilities. Most people agree that getting in touch with our feelings will make us better, more sensitive people, communicators, and writers.

Olfactory/Gustatory Sub-Modalities

Taste and smell, though certainly an integral part of all our experience, are seldom strong influences in the total package of a given state of consciousness. Partly because of their general neutrality, when taste or smell is a noticeable part of an experience, it may be a vitally important one. It may also be a very powerful anchor. Try the following exercise.

Enhancing A State Of Consciousness: Olfactory And Gustatory Adjustments

1. Imagine being with someone you care about and enjoy. Picture the person in your mind and hear the person's voice. Pay attention to your feelings of pleasure.

2. Become aware of the taste in your mouth.

3. Now change it to the taste you have on first waking in the morning, before you've brushed your teeth.

4. Notice any changes in your feelings, your picture, or the sounds you hear.

5. Now change the taste to a more pleasant one, perhaps a peppermint.

6. Notice the corresponding changes in your feelings. Also, be sure you make those tastes and feelings extremely enjoyable before you go any further.

As we said, olfactory and gustatory experiences don't always figure strongly in a state. When they are present, they can be very powerful. If taste or odor is a strong element for you, it may be helpful to make some distinctions in sub-modalities. We know people (including both of us) who reward themselves with chocolate while they're writing. The taste of chocolate has increased their taste for writing.

Olfactory/Gustatory Sub-Modalities

Intensity	Location	Bitter	Sweet
Sour	Salty	Aroma	

Intensity. Soup can illustrate the power of changing intensity of a taste or smell. Imagine eating a delicious bowl of vegetable soup, with just a hint of garlic. What happens to your appetite if the cook has gone overboard with the garlic?

Location. For smell, location is external and related to distance. Where is the smell coming from? For taste, location is a position within the mouth.

Bitter, Sweet, Sour, Salty. The tongue's taste buds register these four tastes. They introduce a whole string of words we use to describe tastes and smells, too: *sharp, pungent, biting*, etc.

Aroma. Some words indicate relatively neutral responses to aroma (*odor, smell*, etc.), but others indicate the quality of response (*fragrance, stench, perfume, effluvia*, etc.). Words like *acrid* indicate quality and intensity of the scent.

Special Care With Sub-Modalities

Just as with the modalities, making a change in one submodality can influence all the others. They all interact, as the following diagram shows:

Figure 3.4
Interaction Of Sub-Modalities

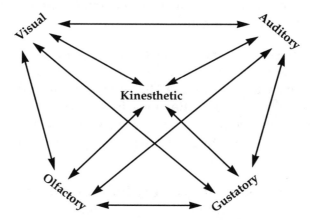

Sometimes people are uncomfortable with the images they make, not because of the content, but because of the form or structure. When you are altering pictures and sounds and trying to juggle several pictures at once, you can easily create unpleasant feelings. Keep in mind the following cautions as you play with your sub-modalities:

- Keep things uncluttered (not too many images crowded into a small space).
- Move images within a picture in the same direction, if it makes sense to do so, and at a comfortable speed.
- Place images at a comfortable distance (not too far away or too close).
- Hold size and intensity to a comfortable degree (not looming too large or glaring too brightly).
- Turn the sound to a comfortable level (not too close, too loud, or too shrill).
- Filter out distracting noises (avoid too many at once).
- Change unpleasant tonalities to more a pleasing sound.
- Make sure you are in a physically comfortable position.
- Breathe comfortably and fully to maintain calm.
- Pay attention to smells and tastes that you may not have been previously aware of.

Each of these elements is a matter of degree and personal preference. However, the reverse of these cautions—too many images moving in different directions, too close, too big, or too bright, and too many sounds at once, too close, too loud, or too shrill, in unpleasant tonalities—are common ways people create anxiety, tension, and a feeling of being overwhelmed. Your pictures and sounds can make big messes in your head just as easily as they can help you, so be gentle with yourself and your feelings.

Defining Your Usual Writing State

Before you begin the process of creating new states, and new anchors, it may be useful to find out what states you create for yourself, now, when you write. Specifically, we want you to spend a few minutes becoming aware of the feelings and experiences you have as you think about beginning a writing project. It may very well be that you already have some built-in anchors that produce just the state you need. Quite likely, though, you may have anchored some states that aren't very useful—like anxiety, frustration, anger, or disgust. Those certainly aren't as productive, or as much fun, as excitement, motivation, and creativity.

Defining Your Usual Writing State

1. Think about the next thing you will need to write: a letter, story, memo, or other project.

2. As you think about it, pay attention to any images that come to mind. What do you see? What are you saying to yourself as you think about this project? Most importantly, how do you feel?

3. When you know the answers to the above questions, take out a pencil and paper, or whatever you usually write with, and begin writing as you normally would on this project, for about ten minutes. When you finish, go to Step 4.

4. Reflect on your writing experience of the last few minutes. What images came to mind during this short time? What have you been saying to yourself? Have these internal processes changed significantly from the last step when you were just thinking about writing? Do you like these internal experiences? Are they the ones you want when you begin a writing project? Could they be better?

Anchors are extremely powerful tools. They are tools, however, only when you are controlling them, rather than the other way around. Your already occurring anchors were created in the same time and place as the memory you use to reproduce them now. In a sense, they were a part of the original experience they recreate. For example, if you learned to feel scared or frustrated every time you had to write for school, you may still feel that way today. In effect, you're still linked to that first experience, like this chain:

Figure 3.5
The Anchoring Chain

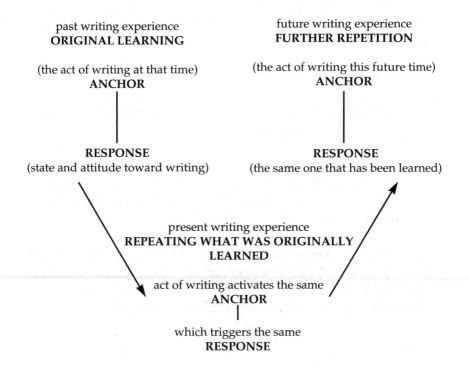

past writing experience
ORIGINAL LEARNING

future writing experience
FURTHER REPETITION

(the act of writing at that time)
ANCHOR

(the act of writing this future time)
ANCHOR

RESPONSE
(state and attitude toward writing)

RESPONSE
(the same one that has been learned)

present writing experience
REPEATING WHAT WAS ORIGINALLY LEARNED

act of writing activates the same
ANCHOR

which triggers the same
RESPONSE

The fact that anchors are accidentally produced artifacts of that long past situation or experience, makes them no less influential. Most important, though, you can change them and create new and equally powerful ones. You can break the chain, like this:

Figure 3.6
Breaking The Anchoring Chain

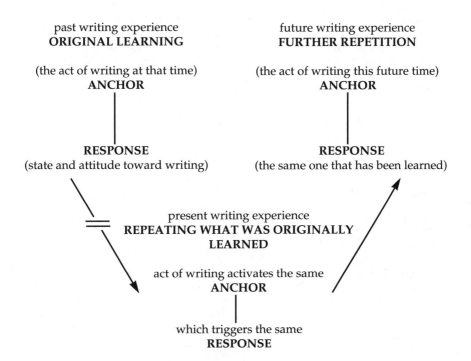

Designing Optimum States

As we consider establishing new anchors, we want to make sure they are anchors for the best possible state for accomplishing what we need. We've created a tool to help you do that, based on what you've learned about sub-modalities. It is a checklist we call a *Designer State Worksheet*. We'll guide you through using it now by going back to that state of excitement and enthusiasm we used before. You may want to copy, or photocopy, the worksheet as it appears here, since you'll be using a number of them. But don't let that slow you down now. We've included a couple of extra blank ones in the Appendix, so if you're ready and eager, go right ahead and use this one now.

Figure 3.7

DESIGNER STATE WORKSHEET

Descriptive Label For State Of Consciousness:

Description Of Content:

Visual Form:

Brightness   Movement/Speed
Size   Location
Color/Black & White   Associated/Disassociated
Distance   Frame/No Frame
3 Dimensional/Flat   Focus
Shape   Clarity
Contrast   Slide/Photo/Motion Picture
Direction   Other?

Auditory Form:

Sounds   Distance
Words   Timbre
Music   Tones
Voices (Whose?)   Pitch
Volume   Location
Duration   Internal/External
Rhythm   Tempo
Other?

Kinesthetic Form:

Emotion   Temperature
Internal   External
Weight   Duration
Size   Pressure
Frequency   Tactile
Proprioceptive   Shape
Movement   Intensity
Moisture   Texture
Rhythm   Balance
Muscle Tension   Breathing
Location
Other?

Olfactory/Gustatory Form:

Sweet   Pungent
Sour   Intensity
Salty   Location
Bitter   Aromatic
Specific Taste   Specific Smell

Anchor:

Using Your Designer State Worksheet

1. Remember that state of excitement and enthusiasm you had earlier, and go back into it now, using your already existing anchor. On a copy you've made of the Designer State Worksheet, on the line at the top that says "Descriptive Label," make a note to help you remember what this state is and what it does for you. You might give it a name like Dyno! or Enthusiastic Excitement, or use a word or phrase that reminds you of that original memory of enthusiasm.

Then fill in a sentence or two on the lines labeled "Description Of Content." These might be notes about the actual images you see and hear, as well as comments about the feelings you have as you look and listen to these images in your mind.

2. Experience this state for a moment and pay close attention to all of the important feelings you have while you're in this state. While you're having these feelings, fill out the KINESTHETIC portion of the worksheet by making notes about the sub-modalities you think are important. The more thorough job you do on this, the more it will help you in the future.

3. Next carefully examine whatever internal visual image you have as you re-experience this special state. Take a moment to fill out the VISUAL portion of the worksheet now, just as you did on the kinesthetic section. Examine the picture in your mind thoroughly enough to make notes on all the sub-modalities you can.

4. Now, pay close attention to the sounds you have in your mind. You may hear your own voice as you talk to yourself about how excited you are. You might hear someone else's voice, perhaps as you heard it in the original experience. Or you might hear other types of sounds as well, from music to bells to fireworks. When you can clearly hear all that is going on in your mind, fill out the AUDITORY portion of the worksheet.

5. If you are aware of any outstanding smells or tastes as you experience this state, make notes about those now as well on the OLFACTORY/GUSTATORY portion of the worksheet.

You now have a complete description of the content and the sub-modalities of your state of enthusiastic excitement. In fact, the worksheet itself could become an anchor for you. In our workshops, we sometimes have people use colored pens to color code or decorate these sheets. The color and decoration, with the notes on the sheet itself, become an anchor for future use.

You've learned how adjusting the sub-modalities can enhance the intensity of a state. As you explored kinesthetic sub-modalities, you used your findings to enhance your state of excitement. When you are designing a specific state, you can use the Designer State Worksheet as a sub-modality checklist, a guide for enhancing each element of the experience, as well as a recording instrument and an anchor. But for now, let's move on to anchoring this and other states more directly.

Establishing New Anchors

What we'd all like, of course, is a firm anchor for retrieving a given, useful, state of consciousness when we want it. Whatever proved the trigger for you in the original exercise of exploring the state of excitement and enthusiasm may be quite dependable, but let's explore ways of establishing anchors. Although almost anything can be an anchor, we generally begin teaching people to anchor themselves by using the sense of touch. A touch is specific enough to be able to duplicate exactly and is therefore the easiest.

Establishing New Anchors

1. Once again, go into your state of enthusiastic excitement.

2. When you get to the height of the *feeling* of excitement, press the tips of your thumb and forefinger together, on your left hand, using gentle but firm pressure. As you do this, you are associating this touch with your experience of excitement, and it will become a part of the total experience.

3. Get up and walk around for a moment to return to a neutral state.

4. Now test your anchor. Sit back down and immediately press your thumb and forefinger together exactly as you did before, using the same touch, the same pressure, etc. Does the feeling of excitement come back? Probably so, at least to some extent.

5. Repeat the entire process several times until the feeling of enthusiastic excitement is just as strong simply from firing your new anchor (touching thumb and forefinger) as it was from your original anchor.

Two points need to be made with regard to kinesthetic, or touch, anchors. First, the touch must be duplicated exactly. For human beings, the proximity and pressure used in a physical touch anchor can be crucial. Even a slight variation may reduce the effectiveness of an anchor considerably for some people.

Second, the point you choose to use as an anchor should be one you don't normally use. If you happen to touch your thumb and forefinger together often, as a habitual gesture, choose some other anchor, perhaps your thumb and some other finger. If the anchor gets associated with many other situations and feelings, it soon becomes neutralized and, therefore, associated with nothing.

To strengthen the anchor, you can give yourself verbal instructions as you fire your anchor. For example, you might say to yourself, "As I touch my thumb and forefinger together, I feel excited and enthusiastic." You can also repeat the anchoring procedure with another similar memory of excitement and enthusiasm. Or you can manipulate the sub-modalities of your memory (make the picture brighter and bigger, or try adding music) to increase the feelings of excitement and enthusiasm.

Another way to strengthen an anchor is to "stack" other related feelings on top of the anchor. Make sure the feelings are compatible, though. If you try to stack opposing feelings, the anchors will cancel each other out. As an example of stacking anchors, let's add creativity to your anchor for excitement and enthusiasm.

Stacking Anchors

1. Go through the steps outlined above to establish an anchor, this time remembering a time when you were especially creative. When you have the experience in mind as vividly as possible, try enhancing it by manipulating the sub-modalities, as you learned earlier.

2. When you're satisfied that you're re-experiencing creativity, anchor the feeling in the same way you anchored the feeling of excitement and enthusiasm. For example, if you touched your thumb and forefinger together then, do it again now, in exactly the same way.

3. Get up and walk around for a moment to return to a neutral state.

4. Now test your anchor. Sit back down and immediately press your thumb and forefinger together exactly as you did before, using the same touch, the same pressure, etc. Do the feelings of creativity and excitement come back?

5. Repeat the entire process several times until the feeling of creativity figures just as strongly in your new anchor (touching thumb and forefinger) as excitement and enthusiasm.

You now have, literally at your fingertips, a terrific tool for overcoming any situations in which you might feel stuck or blocked. Simply use your anchor (put your forefinger and thumb together) to change your state of mind to one more productive. If you like, you can stack as many of these powerful and useful anchors together as you want.

USING ANCHORS

Are you already wondering how many different ways you can use this phenomenon to change yourself and improve your life? The number is almost limitless. If you use your imagination, you can find many things you could change that would make your life more fruitful and enjoyable. We will give you lots more, specifically geared to the writing process, in the next part of this book.

We think it is important for everyone to realize that anchors are an integral part of our daily lives—our patterns of getting up and going to bed are anchors. Each step in our daily routine is an anchor for the next step. In addition to our internal anchors (our routines, our internal pictures, the things we say to ourselves), we have many external anchors: good luck charms, pictures of friends, the way we arrange our belongings. People can also be anchors for certain states of mind. You may know some people who can automatically lift your spirits as soon as you see them. Can you think of some now?

Beyond people and things, though, surroundings themselves become extremely powerful anchors. Intuitively, most of us know this. When we walk into a room we have not been in for some time, most of us find ourselves remembering past experiences in that place. Then we often have the feeling that went with a powerful experience we had there, or maybe just the last time we were there. Think, for example, of your favorite restaurant. One reason these kinds of anchors are so important is that they can be the most limiting. Sometimes when people have had a "bad" experience in some place, they have a hard time going there again. When this happens in the workplace, and they can't seem to "shake" the feelings, work becomes difficult. The same goes for school. As we asked you earlier, where did you learn to write, and how are those memories?

By the same token, good experiences in the workplace, or anywhere else, can make us look forward to going there again. They can also be a constant reminder of the kinds of things and experiences we want in life. Having an environment that is special for writing can make the experience of writing special as well.

Finally, words themselves are anchors. Each word in our language is an anchor for some experience. Since our response to a given word is based on our experience of that word throughout our lives, words sometimes have different meanings to different people. Good writers know how to use words to create certain powerfully meaningful responses in anyone. Good writers know from practice which words trigger what experiences, and they know how to use these anchors.

For example, picture a chair in your mind. That mundane word *chair* can call forth an infinite variety of internal pictures. Was yours an office desk chair, a mahogany ladder-back chair, a leather wing chair, a bentwood rocker, or a Renaissance throne? Take a good look at the chair in your mind. Now, how would you describe it so that someone else could see that same chair?

Good and efficient writers also know how to use anchors for themselves to write more effectively. A picture of Saint Jerome in his study is the trigger for one writer's concentration level for metaphysical writing. Another uses what she calls her writing mantra, a phrase she says to herself that automatically puts her into the state she needs for creating poetry. Throughout the next section of this book, as we lead you through the POWER process of writing, we'll guide you into establishing anchors for useful states of mind in certain phases of writing.

What would it be like for you if you could instantly get yourself into a creative state? How could your life be different if you could automatically get yourself organized? What kinds of states would you most like to be able to have at your fingertips?

Part II

*The
POWER Process*

Chapter Four

Previewing

The Previewing stage of the writing process gives you an overview of the whole communication context. It's that thorough diagram of the situation filled in with your specifics. It's the guidebook that keeps you on course during the rest of the process, that helps you regain your perspective when you get bogged down or discouraged by the details.

In this chapter, we'll explain Previewing in detail and tell you how effective writers do it. Seeing the process work for somebody else can help you feel more comfortable as you use it in your own writing. We'll also take you step by step through Previewing your own writing context—your Self, Purpose, Audience, Code, and Experience. As you develop this picture in your head, you will see yourself beginning to move into your own familiar **POWER space**.

DEFINING *SELF*

We play many roles in our lives, some overlapping, some kept quite separate. Within each role, we express certain facets of our personality more than others. Indeed, human personality is so complex that we cannot possibly express it all at the same time. In most cases, we wouldn't want to. For instance, when you comfort your child after a squabble with a friend over the tricycle, the way you look, sound, and behave projects warmth, love, understanding, and sympathy. When you're enforcing a safety rule, you are firm, fair, and just. The two roles are by no means incompatible, but the situations bring different personality aspects to the foreground. In a larger context, there may be some similarities in your role as parent and your role as supervisor of a beginning sales force. Your expression of these elements at home, however, may be quite different from your expression of them on the job.

As a writer, you bring to your writing all those possibilities for projecting your personality into the task. Start then, with defining your primary role for this particular writing situation. Perhaps you're a dissatisfied customer. This general role has several possible approaches. You could assume an irate role, venting your anger over the damaged merchandise, the store's irresponsibility, the sales staff's ignorance, etc., and generally kindle as many bad feelings in your reader as you had yourself. You could assume a threatening role, stating your demand for a refund and following with threats of calls to the Better Business Bureau and your lawyer. Or you could assume a calm, straightforward manner, describing the problem and requesting your refund.

If your writing situation has several possible approaches, list them, and consider each in turn. Imagine each role, by making a picture in your mind of how you would look, sound, and feel. We'll let Steve's experience demonstrate the process for you.

Steve's *Self*

As part of the upper management team of his company, Steve had to write an important quarterly report. But because he was having a problem defining his role, he procrastinated in writing the report. As division head, he wanted to show his boss how well his group had performed. This, though, was only one goal. As fundraiser, he also wanted to use the report to justify a request for funding of a new venture. Third, as a leader of the team, he wanted to inspire his division to even greater accomplishments for the next quarter. Steve made notes showing details of the three roles he was considering.

Role:	Division Head	Fundraiser	Team Leader
Dress:	sports coat and tie	3-piece suit	shirt sleeves
Attitude:	objective, confident	enthusiastic	progressive, powerful
Feelings:	satisfied, in control	confident	excited

Steve decided to focus on his role as division head reporting to his boss, since that was at the heart of what he had to do. The resulting report could be used later as an appendix to support his request for funds and could be condensed for distribution under a personal cover memo within his division. Steve could have stopped there and produced a good report. But he decided to combine some elements of the team leader into his role of division head. His next notes described his newly defined role:

Role: Division head

Dress: Sport coat and tie

Attitude: Objective and confident, with an undercurrent of excitement. The fact is that we did the job, *and* I'm glad about it.

Feelings: Satisfied, extremely competent, and excited about going on to do even better.

As Steve imagined himself in this role, he adjusted the scene in his mind. He brightened the picture, seeing himself handing the report to his boss in the warm glow of sunlight streaming through the windows. He added his own voice, hearing himself summarizing the report in resonant tones. Then he stepped into the picture, no longer seeing himself, but imagining the scene as if he were really there, and he heightened his own feelings of confidence in the value of his work. He repeated this procedure a few more times, stepping in and out of the picture, making minor adjustments, until he was satisfied with this image of himself.

Your *Self*

Now it's your turn. What role are you playing in the context of this writing task? What is your viewpoint, and why have you chosen this role? If you have some choice here, go through this part of the process with each possibility and then choose the one you like best. You might want to combine several. If you find yourself caught between two incompatible roles, you probably have two different writing tasks, and you need to choose one to do first. The following exercise will help:

Defining Your Self

1.   Imagine you can see and hear yourself in the role you have chosen. This image is disassociated, in third position—not as your audience would see you, but as another person might, from another vantage point. Disassociating from your own image allows you to be more objective, somewhat detached from your feelings.

2.   Next, adjust the way you look and sound in the picture. You may want to change content—setting, clothes, facial expression, etc. Or you may want to alter the form by changing sub-modalities—brighten the light, change the voice tone, speed up or slow down the movement, etc.

3.   When you're satisfied with the picture of yourself, step into it (associate with that image of yourself so you see things through your own eyes, as if you were actually there). Now check your feelings. While "comfortable" may not be an appropriate feeling in our context, you do want to be in as pleasant a state as appropriate (excited, enthusiastic, relaxed, confident, etc.).

   If being in the picture is unpleasant, step back out. See and hear from the outside again, and make whatever adjustments to the picture you think might be helpful. Content changes may be obvious. If not, try changing sub-modalities, one at a time, until things feel "right" to you. Your feelings will let you know when the sights and sounds in your image are the ones you want. Changes in the sub-modalities will cause changes in your feelings. You may want to use one of the Designer State Worksheets as a guide.

4.   Finally, when your role is clarified, anchor it. Probably, the mental image you've been working with has already become a strong anchor. Test it to find out. Another helpful anchor is to give the image of yourself a unique descriptive title. If you're using a worksheet, the worksheet itself may sometimes become an anchor.

When your role is defined, you're ready to join Steve for the second Previewing step.

PINPOINTING YOUR *PURPOSE*

Why are you writing this? What do you want to accomplish? Your purpose may be very clear and straightforward. For example, you may want to make a record of this year's Christmas gifts, given and received, so you don't give your father-in-law another green sweater next year or give the lavender bon-bon dish back to the friend who gave it to you. Sometimes your purpose may be partially decided for you, as in assigned tasks. Perhaps you want to describe some biological process thoroughly enough in your essay exam to convince the teacher you understand it. Often, you'll discover you have several purposes.

Steve's *Purpose*

Steve started out with three purposes: to summarize the quarter's work for his boss, to raise funds for new work, and to inspire his division to more accomplishments. He made reporting to his boss his priority. Then he realized he had multiple purposes within that purpose. His list of purposes follows:

Quarterly Report Purposes
To put the quarter's work into perspective
  To stress accomplishments
  To demonstrate how well we handled problems
  To give the boss the facts she needs for the stockholders
  To impress the boss with my managerial ability

Having pinpointed his specific purposes, Steve made mental images of each of these purposes, seeing the outcome of achieving them. He decided that they were realistic: the report could accomplish them. He also decided they were compatible: one report could do all of them at once.

George's *Purpose*

George's difficulty seemed more serious than Steve's, but his problems resolved themselves when he previewed his writing context. When Dixie met George, he was seriously considering quitting his job rather than continuing to struggle with the report he was trying to write. George was an expert in repairing sophisticated machinery. His new supervisor had asked him for a detailed report on what exactly he did. The machinery he serviced was indeed complicated, and he had pages and pages stuffed with details of its basic care and feeding. Getting all the details down seemed impossible.

Questioned about his purpose, George explained that his supervisor needed to understand how he spent his time so that the supervisor could justify these important costs in the new budget. His former supervisor had hired George and had worked with him for several years. He had known, both from observation and from comparison with former engineers in the position, just how expert George was. The new supervisor, on the other hand, would have only George's report to go on. In fact, he might even include George's report as part of the budget request. George listed these purposes for his report:

Engineering And Maintenance Report Purposes
- Show the importance of regular maintenance.
- Describe how each machine is serviced.
- List all the things that go wrong and what to do.
- Make him see you have to be trained—my job can't be done by somebody you pull in off the street.

George realized that his difficulties stemmed from purposes 2 and 3 in this list. He did, of course, need to give some detail about what he did to back up his other two purposes. But George had been trying to explain his delicate adjustments well enough for the supervisor to follow each movement. He wasn't writing a report; he was trying to write a complete service manual. Once he realized he was attempting more than he needed to, he cut down the task considerably. With his purpose more clearly focused, he wrote the report quickly, supporting his daily activities with a sample maintenance log and reinforcing the importance of his training with a couple of examples of troubleshooting he had just done.

Your *Purpose*

Let's focus now on your purpose. What do you want to accomplish by writing? You may want to make notes in the following exercise, so have your paper and pencil (or pen) handy.

Pinpointing Your Purpose

1. List your purposes for this writing task. They may be business, personal, or both: closing a deal, impressing someone, enhancing a relationship, getting people to take action, solving a problem, creating some sort of experience or feeling, etc. Arrange them by priority.

2. Now question each purpose. Is it worthwhile? Is a written document (letter, report, list, memo, etc.) the most appropriate way to achieve it?

3. Cross-check your purposes if you have more than one or two. Are they compatible, or will you need to write separate documents for some?

4. In your mind, construct a disassociated image of the outcome of your purpose. That is, how will the situation look and sound when you've accomplished your purpose? You may have an image of your reader, perhaps the person who assigned the task, favorably discussing your ideas with others, commending you, or acting differently in some way. You might simply enlarge on the picture you used in defining your role. Shift your attention to the reader and the time frame, to after your writing has been read. What, specifically, do you want to happen as a result of your writing?

5. Next, step into the picture so that you are a participant in the situation with your purpose accomplished. Check your feelings from this vantage point. If things look right and feel right to you from this viewpoint, you probably have a worth-while and well-defined purpose. If you are not comfortable with your Purpose picture, re-examine your purpose itself: is this really what you want? If so, begin to adjust your image of the outcome until it feels "right." Check the content first to be sure your writing has prompted the results you intend. Remember, this is all in your mind, so you can create a picture of your purpose being accomplished perfectly. When the content is right, make whatever sub-modality adjustments you think might help. You might brighten the picture, add more movement, turn up the volume, enhance the color, etc. You could use a Designer State Worksheet to guide these changes.

6.   Anchor this image so that you can recall it later. You could use a kinesthetic anchor, a touch somewhere, the same way you did as you explored anchoring.

Or you could create an auditory anchor. Give your picture a title that reflects your purpose. Then say the title aloud in an appropriate tone of voice. Repeat the title several times, keeping your image firmly in mind. That title, either spoken aloud in that same voice tone or recalled in memory, will anchor your image.

You could use your Designer State Worksheet to create a visual anchor. Write the title of your picture on the Worksheet. Then draw something related to it. Or simply use colored pencils or pens and decorate the page appropriately, while you keep that picture firmly in mind. Now the page itself will call to mind the image of your purpose.

7.   If you have multiple purposes not easily represented in one picture, repeat this exercise with each purpose. When you have pictured all your purposes, see if you can view them all at once or in close sequence.

If you feel strange doing this, you may have conflicting purposes, and you need to resolve the conflict before going much further. Which pictures seem to go together? Which picture doesn't seem to fit with the others? Can you adjust the picture so that it harmonizes with the others, or do you need to address that purpose separately from the others? Frequently, writing separate documents for each purpose resolves the conflict.

IDENTIFYING YOUR *AUDIENCE*

Writing is a solitary task. When we write, the person we're trying to communicate with usually isn't there. Consequently, it's very easy to forget about the other side of the communication model—the reader. Who are you writing for? Will that person read it? All of it? Willingly? Why? What will the reader do with it? Your audience and that person's purpose in reading will have substantial impact on how you write.

Steve's *Audience*

Steve's situation illustrates how our audience influences us. In each of the three roles he considered, he had different audiences. His boss needed the details of what had been done and how, including potential trouble spots. The funding committee needed additional information about the scope and costs of future projects but less detail about how the present quarter's work was actually done. For them, he would down-play trouble spots, both present and future, unless they illustrated a favorable financial point. The people in his division also needed less detail on how work was accomplished, since they had done it themselves, but they needed more praise in the form of favorable comparisons with previous work. They also needed some perspective on the future. As Steve continued with his preview, he filled in an image of his boss reading the report and nodding with approval. He pictured the kinds of actions he'd like the boss to take following her reading of the report, and he imagined her voice asking for the specific details she would need to carry out those actions.

Kay's *Audience*

A fuzzy notion of audience often masks a more fundamental problem involved in multiple audiences. Kay's case is typical. Kay came to one of our workshops struggling with a brochure advertising her services as a body worker, doing therapeutic massage, and as a cosmetologist, improving people's overall appearance. She wanted a brochure for the general public that would include all her services. Her face clearly reflected the strain and confusion she felt.

"General Public" is notoriously hard to satisfy, so we asked her to be more specific about her clients and their needs. Athletes, people with certain ailments, and people wanting stress reduction sought her massage work. Her cosmetology clients were mostly young professional women seeking an improved image. With her years of training and practice, Kay saw these services integrating naturally: an improved body automatically improves a person's image, and a person with an improved image is more likely to take appropriate care of the physical body. But demonstrating this connection and its universal application in one brochure for both kinds of clients was indeed a formidable task.

We suggested two alternatives that put her prospective clients in the foreground. First, she might do two brochures, one for each set of services, designed separately for each audience. Second, she might do a brochure introducing herself as a consultant, with separate inserts describing each of the particular services. She could distribute her brochures, then, by matching them to the kind of people who frequented those places. Once clients responded to the brochure aimed at their obvious needs and got to know her, she could effectively introduce her other services. She realized that a brochure was only an introduction. She would have to educate people about her many services and talents in person. In other words, the brochure might make the introduction, but she'd have to close the sale.

Dee's *Audience*

The way you imagine your audience can make your writing easier or harder. Occasionally, a clear picture of your audience can pose a problem, as it did for Dee. Dee was drafting a master's thesis in psychology and having a very uncomfortable time. She liked her advisor personally but felt she couldn't please him professionally, no matter what she did. Her feelings of intimidation showed in her writing.

She had tried so hard to justify each statement (by including all possible alternative explanations for everything) that it was impossible to tell what she really meant to say, much less actually believed. Worse, she sounded apologetic each time she tried to make a point. Her writing sounded like someone trying to get all her thoughts out, justify them, make excuses or conditions, and finish before anyone else could get a (critical) word in. She wrote very long, run-on sentences, qualifying or apologizing for each detail she brought up.

It turned out that in her mind she was imagining her advisor red-faced with scorn. Each time she wrote a sentence, she saw him looking down at her (literally down) and frowning. She heard his voice scolding her for not being perfect. The more she wrote, the worse his face looked, the nastier he sounded, and the more scared and stuck she felt.

Sid interrupted this self-defeating process. He helped her relax and get comfortable. Then he asked her to talk about her advisor as a person. She felt he was basically a well-meaning person who really cared about her. Once she changed her image of him to a helpful, caring peer, she was much more comfortable, and she could revise her writing appropriately. She also effectively anchored this state of calm so she could use it throughout the project.

Once in a while, you may have to write for a genuinely hostile audience. If seeing your potential attacker in your mind's eye makes you freeze up, we suggest substituting a friendly audience for the first draft. You might imagine presenting a trial version of your document to a helpful editor who will then guide your preparation for the ogre. In the beginning stages of writing, an encouraging audience can often stimulate the flow of your ideas. Later, you'll make whatever adjustments you need for the actual intended reader. If you're at a loss for such an audience, try your mother. If your image of your mother isn't supportive and approving, you're welcome to borrow Dixie's mother.

Your *Audience*

When you are previewing your own writing context, you may be tempted to skip over this step, especially if your audience is a little vague. Don't. When you're talking, it's important to be able to look your listener in the eye. When you're writing, it's equally important to be able to look at your reader in your mind's eye. Remember your past experience with your audience, or with individual representatives. If you don't know any of the people you're writing for, you probably know someone who does, who could tell you what your audience is like and what their needs are. Take time to let the following exercise guide you in understanding and appreciating your audience.

Identifying Your Audience

1.   Write down the name of your primary reader. Or list the people you're writing to. If you are unsure of the names of your audience, write a description, and then choose a person from your own experience as representative of the group. If you really don't know anyone in your audience (are you the one who should be writing this?), make one up. The important thing is to have a person with a face for the next step.

2.   Make a picture in your head of your audience. Again from third position, see yourself, dissociated, talking to this person, presenting your ideas. Put most of your attention on your audience, noticing the kind of response your message is generating. When you say something, does your audience nod, smile, frown, look puzzled? If your listener is not responding as you wish, adjust the picture. Check the content of the picture first—facial expression, posture, body movement, etc. Then use the worksheet to guide your changes in sub-modalities.

3.   Step into the picture now, into first position, so that you seem to be addressing your audience directly. Listen to and watch for responses. When it feels "right," many people describe the feeling as one of confidence or authority as well as relative comfort. Other people add feelings of excitement, power, or motivation. You will have your own personal meaning for these words and your own criteria for that sense of "rightness."

   If you are uncomfortable with the audience you have imagined, step back out of the picture and make whatever adjustments are needed.

4.   When your picture is ready, check the logic of a sequential flow of events—from your audience receiving your message to the accomplishment of your purpose. Begin with your audience accepting the letter (report, etc.), reading it, understanding it, acting on it, and producing some result. Will this person's reading your document lead to the outcome you want? If you cannot imagine the connection between your document and your proposed outcome, you need to rethink (re-imagine) your purpose, your audience, or both.

5.   If your picture is satisfactory, anchor it, perhaps with a key word to describe the picture in your mind or the name of the reader. The image of the reader is often a sufficient anchor. You will refer to your audience throughout the rest of the writing process. If you have only one audience member, you can skip over the rest of this exercise. If you have more than one, go on to step six.

6.   Perhaps you have more than one person as your audience. If you are writing to a fairly homogeneous group, your one representative group member will serve you well. If your group includes several different sorts of readers, you will need to select (create) representatives from each category. In Steve's case, for example, in addition to his mental image of his boss, he also pictured a man from his division with whom he often ate lunch and a person he knew who sometimes provided venture capital.

Another possibility is that you are writing to someone who must then pass your document on to someone else, like the situation with George and his supervisor. This writing through the chain of command is a common situation in the military and in some industries. In this case, you will need to conjure up pictures of each person linking your chain.

7.   Once you have all your necessary audience members clarified, imagine them all sitting in one room listening and responding to you. It's a meeting of the minds, yours and theirs. Make this image disassociated at first; as if you are floating above the group or off to the side, see yourself talking and getting the responses you want from your audience. If you find incompatible members of your audience distracting you (or each other), try adjusting the picture, first in content, then in sub-modalities. (By now you probably know which sub-modalities are likely to make the difference you want.)

If some member of the audience remains recalcitrant or troublesome in any way, you may send that person out of the room. At this point, it's entirely your party, and you can control the guest list. You'll want to consider this person's viewpoint before you complete your document, of course, but that can wait until much later, near the end of the whole process.

8.   When the group looks properly receptive, step into the picture and imagine addressing them directly. Look at them individually and as a group. When the situation feels "right," anchor it.

CLARIFYING YOUR *CODE*

Getting your thoughts and ideas from the point of the light bulb going on inside your head, to the stage of a readable document includes encoding—finding the right language and format. You want your writing to sound right and to look right. Selecting the right level of language comes first. In fact, if you've clarified your role and your audience, you've probably already chosen the appropriate code: technical jargon, for example, for a report to a technician in your field, lay terms for the supervisor outside your field, examples chosen from things familiar to your audience. A manufacturer of medical equipment could refer to model SP-631 to the supervisor of the plant that manufactured it. To the purchasing agent for a hospital, the manufacturer would describe the benefits of the new model sphygmomanometer. At a party, he might be introduced as a maker of blood pressure cuffs. To his four-year-old daughter, he might explain what he makes as a kind of bracelet with a balloon attached that measures what's going on inside people's bodies.

Karen's *Code*

Karen was working in an audio-visual department of a major hospital and nursing school. She wanted to present a set of complaints and recommendations in a letter to her administrator, but she was having difficulty deciding how to say what she thought. She didn't understand why, since she often wrote advertising copy, brochures, pamphlets, scripts, and more.

While visualizing herself talking to her audience during this part of one of our workshops, she suddenly realized the problem. She generally wrote with dramatic images, metaphors, symbols, and allusions. While this code was excellent for the majority of her work, and indeed it was what made her so generally effective, it wouldn't work here. She realized that the administrator thought of her as the "artsy" type, with no real management or organizational skills and, therefore, no useful input. In her mind, she could see the administrator reading what she had written and making a disgusted face, then replying to her in a patronizing tone. This scenario, in fact, had often happened.

The previewing exercise showed her that she needed to sound more "professional" in her letter—to be very specific, brief, direct, and decisive. She shortened her sentences and removed most of the adjectives. She used the same terms she'd heard the administrator use in discussing the situation. She also prepared to support her arguments with references to other papers.

The second big change Karen made in her letter was in format. She decided the business letter form itself was appropriate, rather than an informal memo or a formal report. But within the letter she used lists and headings to make her points stand out.

Your *Code*

Use your previewing situation here. General writing is basically an edited version of talking on paper, so listen to yourself talking or reading your document to your audience. How do you sound? What kind of language are you using? And how is your audience responding? Do you see a look of understanding on your audience's face, or is there some confusion?

Readers see documents before they read them. The way your manuscript looks sets the tone for the reading before the first word is read. Certain formats set up certain expectations. Memos are informal, in-house documents. Letters suggest a little more formality. Reports can be short and informal with a brief cover note or be formal, perhaps several volumes long, with professional binding.

If you're unsure of the appropriate format, ask to see some successful documents of the type you're doing. Do they use headings? Numbered paragraphs? Indentation to show hierarchy? Could some simple changes in layout improve accessibility? Analyze your sample document for style, too. What level of language is used? How long are the sentences? Would a change make it more readable? Then compare your findings with your own task. The following exercise will help you through this coding step.

Clarifying Your Code

1. Call up your picture of your audience and put your finished product in your reader's hands. From the dissociated third position viewpoint, imagine the person actually reading it, in the situation in which it is likely to be read. What kind of design, what sort of format will be easiest to read under those circumstances? Will your reader be expecting it to look a certain way?

2. Now call up the image of your audience as you presented your ideas directly, associated, in First Position. (This is the picture you anchored in the Audience step.) Ask your listener's opinion of what you've been saying.

3. As you listen to the response, pay close attention to the kind of language you hear. Note the vocabulary, the level of technical knowledge evident.

4. Continue a conversation with your audience, matching your language patterns to your audience as much as possible. In situations where your language could not appropriately mirror your audience (you're an adult writing for a child, for example), watch your audience response to make sure your language is understandable and acceptable.

5. Monitor your feelings. If you're uncomfortable or if you notice any discomfort on the part of your imagined audience, make whatever adjustments seem appropriate. Check content first—posture, relative positions, vocabulary choices, etc. Then check sub-modalities, paying special attention here to auditory elements—tonality, pitch, tempo, rhythm, etc. If you haven't been giving the auditory part of your experience much attention, you might want to use the Designer State Worksheet as a checklist. This comfortable conversation between you and your audience guides your code and determines the level of sophistication of your language.

6. If you have several people in your audience, repeat the conversation for each one individually. Then try out the language of one on the other members of the audience, one by one. Determine which kinds of words and which level of sophistication seem to reach all members of the group.

7. Now bring them all back together and address them again as a whole. Listen and watch for responses. Check your feelings again. You want to have that same feeling of confidence and authority as before. (Keep the party fun for yourself as well as for your guests.) When the feeling is "right," you probably have the right code.

ASSESSING YOUR *EXPERIENCE*

The last previewing phase checks your experience against what you want to do. Essentially, you decide whether or not you know what you're talking about and whether you know enough to cover all the points you want to make. If you don't, then you gather the information from whatever sources are appropriate— look it up, make a phone call, go to the library. Experience, for us, includes all pertinent information you have, regardless of how you got it.

In Karen's letter to the hospital administrator, she drew on her personal experience of the problems and her conjectures about possible solutions. She also buttressed her arguments with specific examples she had witnessed, references to other letters, and references to the procedural manual of the hospital.

Once you're sure you have enough information, you must decide which details to include. These decisions will be guided by your previous work in determining your role, purpose, audience, and code. You may have a list of examples, a stack of note cards and highlighted journal articles. Or you may have just a very strong memory of an event. Now you must decide which details will be useful to your audience.

Richard's *Experience*

Richard, a dentist, had a list of his favorite stories illustrating his lecture on dental hygiene for children. He wanted to create a children's booklet for national distribution. He was excited by the contribution he might make to raising tooth-consciousness in both children and their parents. "But," he said, "some of these stories—great when I tell them in my office—don't feel quite right for the booklet, and I don't know how to fix them."

His instincts were right. The troublesome stories involved some local detail, like a flood-zoned playground and a play on Cajun dialect, that would be meaningless to people in another part of the country. Imagining specific members of his audience from other locations listening to the stories helped him understand the problem. He took out the playground and the regional dialect, as well as making other important adjustments. Then his stories came out just fine.

The Research Team's *Experience*

Selection of experience was the root of a problem Dixie mediated between a research team and the division head. "Their reports are irrelevant," complained the head. "He doesn't appreciate the complexity of the situation," fumed the team. The team had done excellent research and always reported it thoroughly— all of it. They hadn't wanted to leave out anything; not only was it all interesting, but you never knew what might eventually be useful if the situation changed. The boss foundered in all the detail for a few pages, unable to find the answer to his immediate question. He gave up reading.

The solution was a change in format, after the team looked back over the code and experience elements of the preview. Knowing what the division head's immediate concern was, they put the concluding information he needed up front in an executive summary. The summary answered his main questions immediately. The discussion section was limited to the primary concern, with the main supporting details each given a heading, so he could quickly locate further details if he needed them. The other information, irrelevant from the division head's present position, was relegated to separate sections or appendices, clearly labeled so that the crucial details could be found easily when the situation changed.

Your *Experience*

The following exercise will show you exactly how to evaluate your experience.

Assessing Your Experience

1. Remember actual experiences you have had with your subject matter. Include library research, conversations, television and radio programs, casual reading, and interviews as well as personal, direct, hands-on encounters. Write down (make a list, draw a flow chart, fill a chalk board, note on note cards, or whatever) everything you can think of about this subject, briefly.

2. Decide which items are relevant to your purpose and to your audience. To check those about which you're hesitant, try them out on your audience. Imagine that you are explaining the first item on your list to your audience, using the appropriate code.

3. Watch and listen for responses. Are you getting what you want? Check for that feeling of confidence to be sure.

4. For items that don't get the response you want, first try adjusting the image—your code, your tone, your body posture, etc. Make notes to yourself, either in your head or on paper, about the details you want to include. If your audience response is still not what you hope for, ask yourself if this item is something really needed. If not, discard that item.

5. If you have several audience members, repeat this process (steps 2-4) for each person.

Check your list now in the light of your purpose. Do you need more information, more examples, more details, to accomplish your goal? Where can you get the experience you need?

7. Gather the remaining necessary information. This careful preview of the whole communication context (your role, purpose, audience, and code) will streamline your research phase, for you won't be side-tracked into gathering irrelevant or inappropriate material. With your self, purpose, audience, and code well-defined, you'll know what information will be valuable.

USING THE PREVIEW *SPACE*

Going through all five elements of the Previewing SPACE has taken a sizeable chunk of space in this book. Is it that important? YES. But after you've done it thoroughly (and with these exercises, you have), the process streamlines itself. In Appendix III: Power POWER User's Guide, we've consolidated all the exercises for each step of the POWER Process. Following each exercise is a set of questions to ask yourself about that step to help clarify your position. The set of questions in the Previewing section, in effect, summarizes the previewing process. Using those questions as you begin a writing task will help you define your SPACE very quickly.

Sid's SPACE Story

Sid discovered the value of previewing the hard way. (He should have met Dixie sooner.) His story may help put the five elements of previewing into perspective.

When Sid began his first book, on NLP and education, his writing experience was limited to college papers and a master's thesis. In his first two chapters, he explained where NLP came from and introduced formal logic and philosophy of science, trying to build credibility for his presentation and to impress people generally—just as he had always done.

He spent several months writing, editing, and polishing. Those two chapters were thorough, concise, cohesive, and very professional. They were also *totally incomprehensible* to anyone without extensive training in philosophy of science, linguistics, or psychology. He felt stupid and couldn't see any way to salvage his hard work. He pushed the project aside for a few months.

When he returned to it, he realized that he had done just what he'd been taught to do for school: impress the instructor with his dazzling insight. He sounded like a wise elderly professor who knew all the fancy phrases but who wasn't concerned with bringing the dawn of comprehension into students' minds. That role is often an effective strategy in writing for college instructors who must read the papers they have assigned, but Sid was no longer writing for a captive audience. And he didn't think anyone—even someone with the requisite background—would read these two chapters voluntarily.

He decided that the problem was simply in the level of language he was using. So he fixed his code by translating what he'd written into plain English. After a couple of months of sporadic work, he proudly reviewed his work. He'd accomplished his goal. Anyone could understand these two chapters with no difficulty.

But something was still wrong. Then it occurred to him that he had two well-written chapters on philosophy, linguistics, and scientific method—for his book on how to help children learn and enjoy school. Terrific. First he had two chapters no one could read. Now he had two chapters no one would care to read. Dejection set in. So did idleness.

Six months later, hoping for a third-time charm, he tried again. This time he did more planning. First, he decided to write as someone who'd been using NLP with children and found some tools that worked, to drop the theoretician role and go at it as someone who'd been in the trenches with the teachers and counselors he wanted to reach. After all, that was why he'd wanted to write the book in the first place.

Thinking of himself as his audiences' peer, a well-defined role (Self), with his Purpose to share new techniques, put his attention on his audiences. He made a list of representative members of the groups he wanted to reach, so he could talk to them in his head. He had clear, specific images in his head of the teachers, counselors, parents, principals, and researchers (Audience) who could use what he had to share (audience Purpose). After all, he'd been doing consulting and training sessions with this audience for a couple of years. He knew them well and had always been received well.

Now he thought about what these people would really want to read: plain English like his second version, to be sure, but without any of the condescending philosophy lessons. Remembering his experiences with training teachers, he recalled their rapt attention when he told stories (Code) of actual kids he'd worked with, complete with successes and blunders.

In thinking about audience and code, he was already sorting through his information and experience (Experience) in his head. He knew that several of his stories always worked well in training sessions and that some of the esoteric material always fell flat. He made lists first. Then he made hard decisions about what to cut.

At last, with a clear preview of his communication context, he knew how to proceed. The first half of his book almost drafted itself. In three months, a publisher had accepted it.

Using Your SPACE

As you've explored the five previewing elements, you've probably noticed how each one relates to the others. Steve's selection of role and primary audience automatically adjusted his purpose, code, and experience choices. Clarifying his audience's need helped George focus his purpose. Karen's assessment of her code not only changed her language and her format but also her own image with her administrator. Sid's attention to his audience and his own image brought his selection of language and detail into line with his purpose.

The same ripple effect is apparent when you use the sub-modalities to improve your SPACE. Adding color to your image of your audience may very well add color to your language. Softening your voice tone may soften any audience resistance and sway them to your way of thinking. Brightening your picture of your Self may light the way to more effective choices of experience, which can brighten your audience receptivity to your ideas.

When the previewing is done, you are well on your way to the actual writing itself. You're probably aware that you've already done lots of mental "writing" during this step. Some of it—your lists and charts—may even already be on paper. But none of it is chiseled in stone. It's a beginning. And beginnings are only beginnings. They can be changed and often will be. Throughout the writing process, you may come back to, rely on, adjust, and refine your SPACE many times. Each time you redefine your SPACE it will be easier, more interesting, and more fun.

Take time to create your SPACE for each writing project, using the questions in the Power POWER User's Guide (Part III, Appendix III) to speed the process. The more time you spend clarifying each element here, the less time the rest of the process will take. In defining your SPACE context, you insure that you won't be stuck in a vacuum. You've made room for the POWER of your communication to happen.

Chapter Five

Organizing

A professional group, asking Dixie to be their meeting speaker, wanted an inspirational talk on technical writing. She chose Genesis 1:1 as her text: "In the beginning God created the heaven and the earth and took six days to get it organized." We make a lot of jokes about getting organized, which shows how important we feel organization is.

Getting our ideas organized is essential to insure that they are received the way we want them to be. Just as importantly, organizing often clarifies our thinking to ourselves. Many people think this is the hardest part of writing, or of almost everything. Actually, previewing your situation could be considered the first step of getting organized. Once your purpose and your reader's purpose are clear, you may find the structure you need is obvious.

In this chapter, we'll tell you about other writers who solved their problems in organizing, and we'll show you some useful tools for speeding the process: getting your brain in gear, finding the right patterns, outlining for perspective, and using plan sheets. Then we'll guide you through the process for yourself.

GETTING YOUR BRAIN IN GEAR

The popular press has made much of "left brain" and "right brain" kinds of thinking. The left half of the cerebral cortex is largely responsible for sequential, ordered, linear, "rational" types of information processing. The right half takes care of complex connections between different kinds and levels of information, the "creative" activity. Actually, we use both halves of the cortex as well as other parts of the brain for just about all our thought processing. If you do one kind of thinking better than another, it doesn't mean half of your brain is underdeveloped; it just means it's underused. In other words, you need practice. Rather than thinking about a task, or yourself, as left-brained or right-brained, think about using your whole brain and becoming fully creative, functional, and efficient.

Working with ideas demands whole-brain thinking. Many people, however, seem to have difficulty integrating these divergent kinds of thinking. We seem to switch modes when going from a "left-brain task" to a "right-brain task." For example, reading a novel for pleasure is a different sort of task from taking it apart structurally to see how the author made it work. The same goes for viewing a painting as a whole and paying attention to our emotional response to it, as compared to studying the techniques the artist used in creating it. Switching from one kind of task to another takes a shift in consciousness. If you find the shift jolting, be gentle with your brain and do one thing at a time.

The internal strategies we teach are designed to take individual differences and needs into account. There is no one "best" way to go about organizing information. Both halves of the brain will be needed, each in its proper time. Fortunately, the brain knows this. All we have to do is get in the proper frame of mind to allow the brain to work.

You've probably experienced that frame of mind before, perhaps in another context. If you've had it before, or can imagine it, you can have it again. And the exercise we'll take you through in a few pages will help you get that frame of mind anchored so that you can use your organizational talents when you need them.

Steve's Organizing State Of Mind

Steve wanted the organization of his quarterly report to reflect his managerial talent. He wanted his division head to find his report easy to use, easy to reference later. He'd never quite gotten that quality of structure in any of his previous writing. As he thought about the state of mind in general, he remembered the time he'd reorganized his clothes, from socks to shirts, so that he could find things even in the dark. He'd done it so well that whoever did the laundry, he himself, his wife, or any of the children, could tell at a glance what went where. That's what he wanted. He used our Designer State Worksheet to fill out the details of his memory, and then he anchored the state of mind for writing his report. Here are the notes from his worksheet.

Steve's Designer State Worksheet

Content: I'm the Wardrobe Engineer—Super-Organizer!

Visual form: The picture—me placing and directing things to place themselves—is bright and clear, in color, moving. I'm there, being the Super-hero.

Auditory form: I hear my voice, saying things like "this goes there, and this here." I sound confident, certain, almost commanding. The volume is loud enough to direct the items I'm sorting, but not loud enough to disturb anybody in another room.

Kinesthetic form: I feel great! relaxed but full of energy, especially in the pit of my stomach. As I move, it's almost like dancing— maybe a rumba. I can feel my weight perfectly balanced on the balls of my feet.

Your Organizing State

You can probably remember times when you felt scattered and disorganized. By contrast, it's likely you can also remember what it is like to be cool, efficient, and step-by-step in your thinking. This second state of mind is the one we want to have on tap when we need it.

Setting Your State Of Mind For Organizing

1. Begin by remembering a time when you were a cool, logical, orderly thinker. You may have been writing at the time, but it isn't necessary to have an example that involves writing at all.

If you have difficulty thinking of a time, review your favorite activities that call for structure—cooking, dancing, repairing engines, playing sports, etc. Or think about those Escher drawings that create ambiguous images: you look at one and see black birds flying to the right, and then, as you continue to look, your perception shifts so that you see white birds flying to the left. You've recognized a new pattern.

If you still can't imagine yourself as an organized thinker, imagine someone else who is. Then pretend that you are that person. Go through this step imagining that you are this organized clear thinker. "As if" works fine.

2.   When you have remembered a time of organized clear thinking, pay attention to the image in your mind. Make sure you are associated with the image this time. That is, see things as you saw them, and look around at the setting as you did at the time. Notice the sounds you hear, the same sounds you heard then, both externally and inside your head.

3.   Shift your attention to your feelings now. Make sure you have the feeling of being organized and efficient.

4.   Use the worksheet list of sub-modalities as a guide to enhance the feeling. Adjust your image until your feelings of being organized are optimal.

5.   Anchor this state of mind. You'll find it helpful often.

6.   In this state of mind, turn your attention to your writing project. Often a pattern suitable for your SPACE will be immediately apparent. If no pattern suggests itself, read on into the next section of this chapter. Then return to this step.

7.   Make notes to yourself about the patterns that best suit your SPACE. These notes are for you, not your audience and will guide you in the next POWER step. Another section in this chapter offers suggestions about how to make those notes.

Just getting into an organized state of mind is all some people need to organize information. The rest of the process seems to flow automatically, especially when they look back at their preview of self, purpose, audience, code, and experience. Most people, though, also make conscious use of other organizational tools.

FINDING THE RIGHT PATTERNS

When you're stalled in organizing a body of data, you may find yourself saying one of two things:
"This is too much data to deal with!"
"I can't decide where to start!"

Using a checklist like the one that follows of some of the most common patterns of organization will give you both a place to start and a way to manipulate your information into manageable size.

Chunking down (looking for smaller units within the whole) is usually the easiest way to begin. Ask yourself the following questions:

Is there any part of this information that...
- needs chronological narration?
- needs spatial description?
- could use an illustration or example?
- could be compared or contrasted?
- an analogy would clarify?
- should be classified?
- needs one of the process patterns?
- analyzes a cause/effect relationship?
- must be defined?

When you find a chunk of data that calls for one of these organizational patterns, then ask the same questions about that chunk. That is, look for a smaller chunk of information within that data.

While breaking the information into smaller units of data is a good beginning, you may want to chunk up, too. As you look at the smaller units, ask what patterns could be made when you fit them together.

The patterns included in the checklist above are among those described by rhetoricians over the centuries, patterns of organization that recur as human beings make use of information. Ideally, the organizational pattern you choose will reflect the integral relationship of your information and your purpose. Sometimes just a review of these patterns can nudge you into seeing the most logical structure for what you're dealing with, finding the form that fits the function. If you're unfamiliar with these patterns, here's a brief summary of what they can do for you.

Chronological (Time) Pattern

In a chronological, or narrative, approach, the message is presented in the sequence in which it occurred in time. It is most commonly used in storytelling and in the experimental section of a report. Choose chronological order when *sequence* of events is more important than any other element.

Spatial (Place) Pattern

Use spatial order for descriptions of things, places, or organizational structure. Be sure to give your reader cues about the relationship of details (at the top, from left to right, etc.). Spatial order may also help in discussing a diagram, photograph, or other graphic aid.

Illustrative Pattern

Illustrations, or examples, make the abstract more concrete and so more accessible to the reader. This very elastic pattern can control a whole report or can be complete in one sentence. In using this pattern, you must ask two questions: how many examples do I need? and how fully developed should those examples be?

To answer both questions, consider your audience. You want to give enough examples to illustrate your point and make it specific. A well-informed audience may need only one general example. An uninformed or lay audience will need more examples or more detailed development of an example.

Be sure to relate the example to your point. Your audience might be asking such questions as why this example? what does it illustrate? how is it like (or different from) another example?

Comparison-Contrast Pattern

Use this pattern when two or more things must be compared, for instance, in recommending purchase of one over the other or of both rather than just one. Actually, comparison-contrast is three patterns.

Parallel Order Or Whole By Whole

In parallel order or whole by whole, you tell everything about the first thing and then tell everything about the second thing, usually following the same order of points about each. Use this one when the comparisons are brief. An outline would look like this:

Thing 1
    Point A
    Point B
    Point C

Thing 2
    Point A
    Point B
    Point C

Alternating Or Part By Part

In alternating or part by part, you describe one aspect about the first thing and then describe that same aspect about the second thing. Then you proceed to the second aspect of the two things, and so on. Use this pattern when your comparisons are long and detailed. An outline would look like this:

Point A
    Thing 1
    Thing 2

Point B
    Thing 1
    Thing 2

Point C
    Thing 1
    Thing 2

Likeness-Difference Or Known-Unknown

In likeness-difference or known-unknown, you describe the like aspects of the two things and then their differences, or the known (to your audience) and then the unknown. This pattern is really a meta-pattern for the first two. That is, within the broader framework of likenesses, you will choose to discuss them whether by parallel order or by alternating from one thing to the other. An outline might look like this:

> Likenesses
>> Point A
>> Point C
>>> Thing 1
>>> Thing 2
>
> Differences
>> Point B
>>> Thing 1
>>> Thing 2

In preparing to use a comparison-contrast pattern, you might consider these questions:

- What is the basis for comparison?
- Is there significant common ground to make the comparison useful?
- Do similarities and differences line up neatly, or are points of comparison scattered?

Using a comparison grid like the one shown in the planning device section of this chapter may be helpful in answering these questions. A visual aid of a similar sort may be helpful to your reader, too.

Analogy Pattern

Analogy is a special kind of comparison in which a striking similarity between two things becomes the basis for comparison, even though the two things may be unlike in any other way (e.g. the monarch butterfly's wings are like a stained glass window).

This pattern helps clarify an abstraction or something completely new and unknown by relating it to something concrete and familiar. It is especially useful in explaining a technical topic to a lay audience. Although it can be invaluable in an explanation, in an argument you may use it for clarification only; it is invalid as proof.

Classification Pattern

Classification groups together things that are alike in some particular way. Three rules for setting up a classification system lead to a convenient formula:

1. Every classification must be made on one clear and consistent basis. A wardrobe consultant could, for example, classify clients on the basis of current hair color.

2. If a class is subdivided, there must be at least two subdivisions. Hair color can be subdivided into more than two categories.

3. The classification system must be able to handle all items in a given body of data. Current hair color will prove an inadequate basis for classification the first time our wardrobe consultant has a bald client.

Formula: X (group of data) may be divided into Y (number) of classes on the basis of Z (primary point of comparison).

Example: The readers of this book may be divided into two groups on the basis of sex.

Process Patterns

In using a process pattern, first make sure you know the process thoroughly. Then divide it into steps, and explain each step with enough detail that your audience can easily follow. There are actually four types of process explanations:

How-It-Works

How-it-works explains a process, usually with a chronological order, so that the reader can understand how something happens. This pattern makes a good pre-test study review over large chunks of material. For instance, if you've been studying organs of the body, put them together to see how digestion works. Trace the progress of a new law proposal though the three components of the American legislative system to show how the system works.

How-To-Do-It

How-to-do-it gives instructions so that the reader can then perform the process. Audience analysis is especially important here. You don't want to get bogged down in trivia, but you want to be sure you're giving enough information so the audience will really know *how* to do it, not merely *what* to do.

How-It-Is-Organized

How-it-is-organized uses functional order (as in departments of a business) or spatial order to explain the structure of something.

How-It-Happened

How-it-happened explains the cause of some known effect.

Causal Analysis Pattern

Causal analysis is really a particular kind of the how-it-happened process pattern. In it, some process is broken into parts to demonstrate a causal relationship.

To discover the cause of a given effect is a common problem. However, we must often settle for probable cause. In any case, in using this pattern, be sure to *demonstrate*, not merely assert, the relationship between the cause and the effect.

For simple cause-to-effect or effect-to-cause relationships, a standard outline will suffice. For complicated patterns of multiple causes or effects or of chain reactions, visuals may help:

Figure 5.1
Cause-Effect Visuals

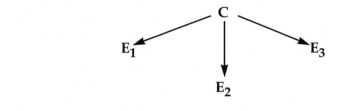

Definition Pattern

Definitions often use illustration, comparison-contrast, analogy, and classification in their development. A bare-boned classical definition has three parts:

1. The *term* is the thing you are defining.
2. The *genus* is the general class of things to which it belongs.
3. The *differentia* are those characteristics that make it different from all other members of that class.

Take that third definition of parts as an example. The *term* is "differentia," the *genus* is "characteristics," and the *differentia* are "that make it different from all other" characteristics.

In defining something, keep in mind these cautions:

- Be as clear and simple as possible. Avoid ambiguity, highly figurative language, or obfuscation.
- Term and genus should be in the same part of speech—e.g. a dredge (noun) is a machine (noun) that... Especially avoid "is where" or "is when" constructions.
- Be positive. To say what something is *not* may be helpful as a beginning point, but be sure to follow that with an explanation of what it *is*.

The Place For Patterns

Nobody, outside of an old-fashioned school setting, ever sits down saying, "I think I'll write an essay of definition." The organizational pattern you choose for your writing must grow out of what you have to say and the context you say it in. Moreover, in anything longer than a paragraph, rarely is any one pattern used exclusively. One may dominate overall, but you'll use others to help develop your ideas. Still, being aware of the patterns in and of themselves can make it easier to spot the logical organization inherent in your topic and your communication context.

OUTLINING FOR PERSPECTIVE

If you don't like outlining, you may simply be trying to use the wrong kind of outline.

Perhaps you remember when you were first learning to write essays and answers to discussion questions. Your teacher may have told you something like this: "Think about your topic, make an outline, write your first draft, and then polish it. I'll want you to hand in your outline with your finished essay."

So you did as you were directed. You thought, outlined, wrote, thought again, revised, polished, and handed in a magnificent piece of work. Your paper was returned with this note: "Your essay is interesting and original, but it doesn't match your outline. **F.**" Well. You certainly learned that lesson. Thereafter, you wrote your essay and *then* wrote your outline. Right?

The problem is that your teacher had confused two distinct purposes for outlines. The teacher asked for a writer's outline but expected to get an outline for the reader. And those two outlines can sometimes be very different.

Two Purposes For Outlines

A writer outlining is rather like a vacationer planning a trip to a new place. You make plans about where you want to go, what you want to see and do. And you make guesses about how long each travel chunk and each event will take. If you don't make plans, you may still have a wonderful vacation, but you'll probably miss out on a lot of things.

Vacations seldom work out exactly as planned, though. Along the way you discover that one attraction you wanted to see is closed. But just next door is an unadvertised quaint little restaurant with a petting zoo in the backyard. And so it goes; some things work as predicted, others don't work out, and you discover new adventure possibilities. So it is with writing. You discover that one example doesn't work, but you find two more that are better anyway. Someone tells you about a new development that could influence the outcome of your topic. You take advantage of whatever happens in the process.

Now your vacation is over. Your tales and slide show are so good that your best friend wants to do just what you did. Would you please write up a guide? You planned your vacation making some guesses. Now you've been there and can report the actual territory. The same goes with writing. When you plan your writing, you're making predictions about where you will go with your argument. When you finish the writing, you can make a more exact guide for a reader, an outline to aid someone in navigating the intricacies of your thinking.

Your writing may be complex enough that the reader needs an outline. A table of contents, however, may serve the same function. More often, headings or clear topic sentences will suffice. That decision, though, is one you will make later. For now in the writing process, though you have your reader's needs and purposes in mind, you are primarily concerned with organizing for yourself.

How Outlining Helps

Outlining for a writer has two main functions. To clarify the first function, take a look at these two pictures:

Figure 5.2
Street Scene A

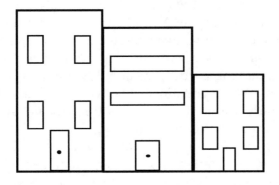

Figure 5.3
Street Scene B

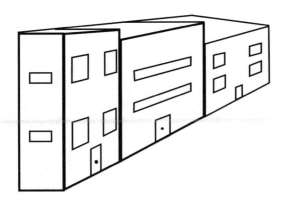

In Street Scene A, the spatial relationships of the buildings and trees aren't clear. Street Scene B has depth, perspective. The artist's technique for creating perspective is to choose a point on the horizon, a vanishing point, and make all the lines that are parallel in the third dimension move toward that point, as Figure 5.4 illustrates:

Figure 5.4
Creating Perspective In Street Scene B

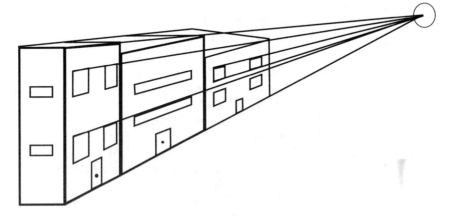

With that in mind, now take a look at a traditional outline. The ideas that are on the same plane, the same hierarchy, are lined up directly under each other. The supporting ideas for each point are indented to show their relationship to each other and to the main idea. The slanted lines follow the indentations and connecting main points to subpoints are like the lines illustrating the slant of the horizontal planes to increase perspective.

Figure 5.5
Perspective In An Outline

Formal Outline Conventions

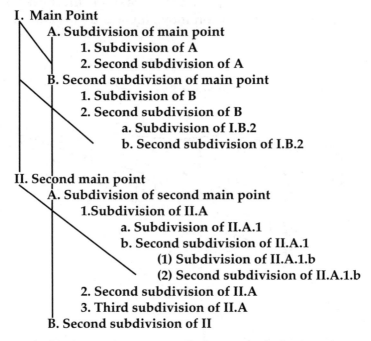

I. Main Point
   A. Subdivision of main point
      1. Subdivision of A
      2. Second subdivision of A
   B. Second subdivision of main point
      1. Subdivision of B
      2. Second subdivision of B
         a. Subdivision of I.B.2
         b. Second subdivision of I.B.2

II. Second main point
   A. Subdivision of second main point
      1.Subdivision of II.A
         a. Subdivision of II.A.1
         b. Second subdivision of II.A.1
            (1) Subdivision of II.A.1.b
            (2) Second subdivision of II.A.1.b
      2. Second subdivision of II.A
      3. Third subdivision of II.A
   B. Second subdivision of II

A mass of information can easily be overwhelming. An outline helps you put it in perspective.

A second purpose for a writer's outline is to trap ideas when they occur. Perhaps you've had the experience of thinking of the perfect example to use in a later point in your writing, and you said to yourself, "I'll be sure to remember that when I get to that section." Later you found yourself saying, "Now what was that great idea I had?" A note at the appropriate point in your outline will make sure that idea is available when you're ready for it. Ideas stay in the trap, however, only if you actually do put them there. Don't worry about messing up your outline page; make a note to yourself on the outline immediately when the idea pops up.

The Shape Of An Outline

Some people object to outlining because they don't want to have to deal with when to use Roman or Arabic numerals and capital or lower case letters or because all the decimals or zeros of other systems are confusing. You may also recall a teacher's saying, "If you have an *A*, you'll have to have a *B*." Maybe you had only one *A* example, so you left it out, since you didn't have a *B*. It seemed as if you had to make what you said fit the outline structure, rather than having the outline help you say what you wanted to say.

Again, here's some confusion between the writer's outline and the reader's. The careful numbering system enables you to refer a reader to the outline from some part of the text. Attention to parallel and balanced structure dramatizes the full development of ideas. But the writer getting organized really needn't bother with those conventions. The indentations on the page will keep your perspective perfectly well without the numbering, as in the following illustration.

Figure 5.6
Informal Perspective Outline

> Informal outlines
> > Jotted notes
> > Analysis of brainstorming
> > Proposition tree
> > Flow charts, grids
> > Variations on formal patterns
> > > Unmarked patterns
> > > Incomplete patterns
>
> Formal outlines
> > Perspective outlines
> > > Sentence outlines
> > > Topic outlines
> > Non-perspective outlines
> > > Paragraph outlines
> > > Lists

And now we'd like you to expand your definition of outline. Remember its purpose: it's a guide to unknown territory (you haven't written anything yet, so you don't know what will actually be there), a tool to help you keep your ideas in perspective. Any configuration that gives you a visual map of the relationship of your ideas is an outline. A flow chart may be the best way to outline some information. For organizing complex procedures, a PERT or CPM chart or a Gantt time line may be the clearest kind of outline (and may be the clearest way of presenting your data, too). Outline diagrams don't have to conform to any pattern except the relation of ideas you're dealing with. Here's an outline Dixie used for a speech, the arrows reminding her at a glance of the points she wanted to make about the dynamics of the relationships involved.

Figure 5.7
Speech Dynamics Outline

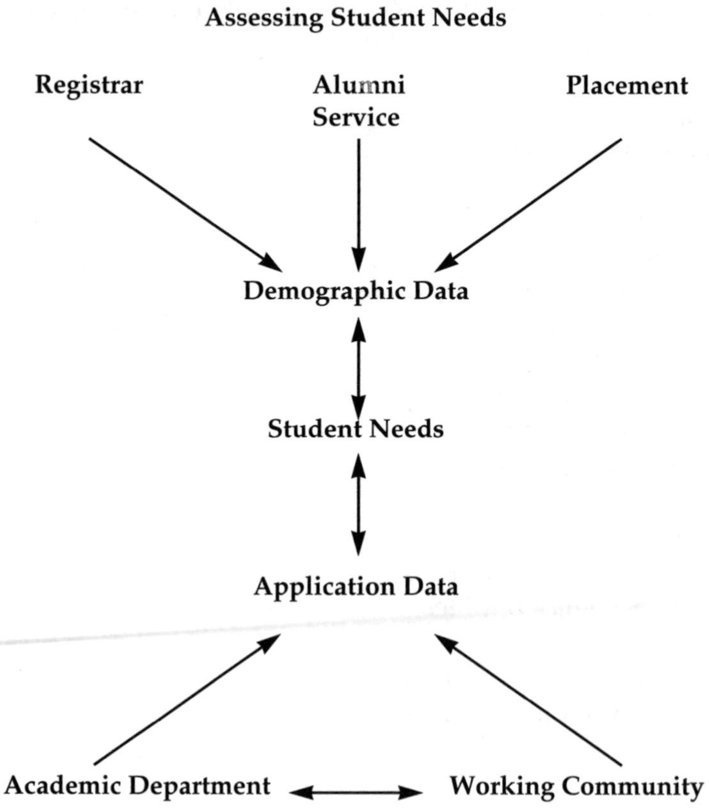

Assessing Student Needs

| Registrar | Alumni Service | Placement |

Demographic Data

Student Needs

Application Data

Academic Department ⟷ **Working Community**

Sid used an even less formal system to organize his first book: the old matching test game. He had listed all the techniques he wanted to teach when he was defining his purpose. In previewing his experience, he had listed all the stories he used in his workshops, the ones that always held people's attention. Then he drew lines from the techniques to the stories that illustrated them.

Some of his stories illustrated several points. So he split the stories into parts, each part teaching one major point. Next, he numbered the points in the best order for learning. And that became the outline for the first part of his book.

The second part of his book was to be exercises and experiments for readers to actually try out the techniques. He organized it the same way. He listed all the exercises he'd used in his workshops, circled the best ones for doing by yourself, and drew lines from those to the techniques they taught. Voila! Part II was practically done!

In sum, there are two things to remember about outlines. First, they always help. It's easier to get someplace (like to the end of your writing task) if you have some perspective on how to get there. Second, they rarely ever turn out to be exact. Like the vacation, things change as you write. And getting organized is not the end of the process.

PLANNING DEVICES: ALTERNATIVES TO OUTLINING

Outlines are only one format for helping you get perspective on your information and get it organized. Here are a few examples of other varieties of planning devices, with suggestions about developing your own, suited specifically to the kind of planning and writing you need to do.

Plan Sheets

One of the handiest tools for getting organized is a plan sheet, an idea pioneered in technical writing by John Harris at Brigham Young University. Its basic elements include logistical data (when the report is due, etc.), an overview of the context (writer's role, purpose, reader), and details about the content. Dixie uses the generic plan sheet in Figure 5.8 with many of her clients in industry.

Figure 5.8
Generic Plan Sheet For Reports

REPORT WORKSHEET

Writer: (position)   Date Assigned:
Subject: Date Due:
Title:

Reader (person assumed to actually use information presented)
Technical level (education, knowledge of topic, experience, etc.):

Position (job title and/or organizational relationship to writer):

Attitude toward subject (interested, hostile, etc.):

Other factors:

Secondary readers (others who will see the report or parts of it):

Reader's Purpose
Why will the reader read the report?

What should the reader know after reading?

What should the reader be able to do after reading?

Writer's Purpose
Primary purpose(s) (to persuade, change attitude, inform, etc.):

Secondary purpose(s) (to make money, boost ego, get promotions, etc):

Scope and Plan
Source materials (direct study, personal observation, library, etc.):

Primary organization (definition, causal analysis, narrative, etc.):

Available aids (visuals, tables, etc.):

Format
Standard format for this report:

Adaptations of standard format needed:

When the plan sheet is completed, the writer has completed steps one and two of the POWER process, previewing and organizing, all on one sheet. You can make a plan sheet for any writing task. This one, for a technical report, assumes the writer has little difficulty with organizing after the Previewing is done, so very little space is given to content per se.

The next plan sheet example in Figure 5.9, a task analysis worksheet, is based on one designed by Donald H. Cunningham and Thomas E. Pearsall, two leaders in the field of technical writing. Specifically for writing instructions, it combines a brief audience analysis with an outline of content.

Figure 5.9
Task Analysis Worksheet

Task Objective (What will the reader do?):

Who performs the Task?:

Performance Circumstances:

Equipment Needed:

Material Needed:

No.	Steps in Performing the Task	Precautions	Graphics	Learning Difficulties

This Plan Sheet For Questionnaire in Figure 5.10 includes an editing check list to guide the question-writing and also to help with evaluating and revising:

Figure 5.10

PLAN SHEET FOR QUESTIONNAIRE

TOPIC TO BE INVESTIGATED:

PURPOSE OF THE QUESTIONNAIRE:

　　What information is sought?

　　Who has that information?

　　What will be done with the information?

　　How accurate must the data be?

POPULATION TO BE SURVEYED:

METHOD OF DISTRIBUTION AND COLLECTION:

CHECK LIST FOR QUESTIONNAIRE CONSTRUCTION

QUESTIONS
　　Does each question elicit necessary information?

　　Are there enough questions to get all the information needed?

　　Does each question cover only one item?

　　Is the language of each question clear and appropriate?

INSTRUCTIONS
　　Does the questionnaire begin with a set of instructions for answering?

　　Are the instructions explicit and brief?

FORMAT
　　Does the questionnaire present a pleasant appearance?

　　Is there sufficient space for answers?

　　Will the layout permit efficient tabulation of data?

This next plan sheet in Figure 5.11 Dixie developed for a real estate agent whose job included investigating complaints from apartment dwellers about their neighbors as well as their own dwellings.

Figure 5.11

COMPLAINT INVESTIGATION REPORT PLAN SHEET

COMPLAINTANT'S NAME: DATE:

NATURE OF COMPLAINT:

DATE OF INVESTIGATION: TIME:

SITE OBSERVATIONS:

Physical Evidence:

Damage Assessment:

DIAGRAM(S) OR PICTURE(S) NEEDED:

PERSON(S) INTERVIEWED:

INTERVIEW FACTS: SOURCE(S:)

ACTION(S) TAKEN:

FOLLOW-UP NEEDED:

RECOMMENDATIONS:

This last plan sheet is one Dixie gives clients for writing job application letters:

Figure 5.12

JOB COVER LETTER PLAN SHEET

EMPLOYER'S NAME:

EMPLOYER'S ADDRESS:

JOB TITLE:

JOB QUALIFICATIONS (WHAT, SPECIFICALLY, DO THEY NEED?):

MATCHING QUALIFICATIONS ON YOUR RESUME:

MATCHING QUALIFICATIONS NOT SHOWN ON YOUR RESUME:

ACTION REQUEST:

The best plan sheets are tailored to the specific demands of a writing task. With your previewing in mind, you can easily make the notes about audience and purpose. Then list elements that must be included to satisfy the purpose. List any problems that might occur, or warning spots, and make notes about ways to head off the trouble. Though originally intended for technical reports, Dixie has adapted the plan sheet idea for tasks ranging from institutional self-studies and business sales letters, to beginning writers' paragraph development and high-school graduate thank you notes.

These examples have indicated the variety of applications possible. We hope you've started thinking about how you can develop your own plan sheet. As you think about the writing you routinely do, you probably notice some patterns. Certain kinds of writing always need certain kinds of information, for example. Or you may notice that you routinely skip certain aspects of a report unless you're reminded of them. Put those details on your plan sheet. Most importantly, be sure to include the kinds of fill-in categories that help you keep in mind the other side of the communication context: your reader.

A plan sheet has two major advantages. First, it puts the communication context right up front where the writer can be reminded frequently. Second, its preplanned slots eliminate any foundering over where to start; you just fill in the blanks. For people who are intimidated by a blank page, it's wonderful. You start with a page that already has something on it, and by the time you've filled in the details called for, you're well into beginning your first draft.

Comparison/Contrast Grid

The comparison/contrast grid, Figure 5.13, is a chart that puts all the information you have about the items you are comparing together in one place so that you can see relationships among the parts more clearly. The grid is usually a preliminary to an outline. However, when the comparative elements balance neatly, the grid itself may be all the outline you need.

Figure 5.13
Comparison/Contrast Grid

Items to be compared

Points of comparison

Tree Diagrams And Other Mapping Techniques

Tree diagrams and other mapping techniques help you see relationships among ideas. Tree diagrams work from a general idea to a specific focus. Other patterns begin with a specific idea and map the details that support the idea.

Try the tree diagram as you explore your ideas about a topic, in that early stage of writing when you're still clarifying your own thoughts. It's especially useful when you have a general topic you want to talk or write about but haven't decided which slant or which aspect you want to develop. Begin with your general topic. Then think how many ways you could branch out from there. Which of those branches might be worth exploring further? The tree diagram in Figure 5.14 helped Dixie develop first an inspirational talk and later a self-help book on meditation.

Figure 5.14
Tree Diagram

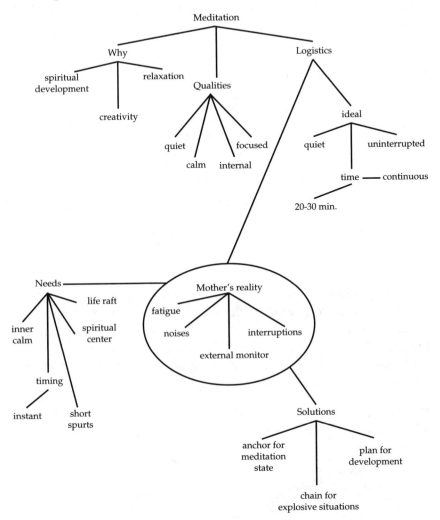

Try a mapping technique when the topic already has some kind of coherent development. Handy for your own organizing, mapping patterns can be even more useful when you're taking notes on a speaker. Having the complete summary of a speech, lecture, or chapter in a book on one page, with the relationship of parts clearly indicated, is an excellent study device and memory jogger. You won't get the detail you might have in an outline, but the graphic layout often makes up for that.

The example map in Figure 5.15 is appropriate when you know where the speaker is going with the topic. You proceed down the road of the speech, noting the important sights on the tour.

Figure 5.15
Street Map Of Speech

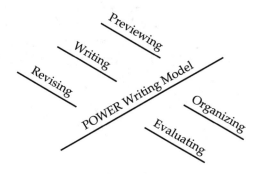

If a speaker gives you no initial clues about organizational structure, or if you want to develop a topic so that all the inter-linking aspects are clear, try the town square map, illustrated in Figure 5.16. Put your topic in the middle of the page, let your ideas lead off the square (or wheel spokes, or spider web center), and draw in the side streets.

Figure 5.16
Town Square Map Of Speech

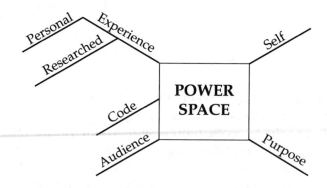

CPM, PERT Charts And Other Time Management Techniques

Efficiency experts have developed all sorts of time management devices, including a variety of visual representations, to help people organize their projects and their lives. People in management and engineering routinely use many of them. Some of these graphic outlines are appropriate for writing tasks, too. Critical Path Method (CPM) helps set priorities when several tasks are progressing at the same time. You might find it helps you keep track of your main characters when you have multiple plots going, just as much as it helps your children streamline their morning routine for getting off to school. Program Evaluation Review Technique (PERT Charts) and the Gantt time line are helpful for collaborative projects or for people juggling writing with other activities. If you already use these devices in your business, enjoy exploring their applications for the rest of your life.

Story Boards

Story boards can be a lot of fun as well as good organizing tools. These are actually cartoons, just like in the Sunday comics, that outline the steps in your narrative. This technique is very commonly used in both film making and all forms of advertising.

Simply, the idea is to actually sketch a cartoon frame for each step in whatever process you are developing or writing about. If you were making a movie, each scene could have its own frame, or even several frames, one for each camera angle. In advertising, especially the creation of television commercials, each frame could present an idea about the product that the producers most wish to emphasize. Once each frame is designed, they are placed in the chronological order in which they will appear, on a board or a wall if there are lots of them. The result is a visual guide, step by step, through the proposed material.

Even if you are not making movies or commercials, story boarding can be a very useful tool. It is applicable in any process which people have a set of tasks or a series of events, that have to proceed in a certain order. For example, Sid uses this concept whenever he devises an exercise for people to follow, like the ones in this book. Since he doesn't draw much better than an infant, he has adapted the process. Instead of drawing out separate frames, he visualizes people going though each step in the process. He also breaks the process down into smaller and smaller pieces to insure that each step is clear and logical. A gap in the pictures shows him where his exercise needs further development.

In addition to writing for other media, fiction, or advertising, you might consider using story boards to help you organize any detailed instructional material. It is also useful in nearly all business correspondence. And you might find it helpful in guiding your creativity. As an experiment, try doing a story board of your own activities while you go through some detailed process you are good at. Find out how much this technique can help you fill in missing details and re-order the steps, if necessary. It may also help you figure out what makes you so good at it.

PERSPECTIVE ON THE PROCESS

Getting organized is certainly important. And just as this stage goes more easily if you've done a good job with previewing the situation, the more smoothly the subsequent stages of writing will go. Still, don't let yourself get hung up on organization. Many people like to write out everything and then organize it. Generally, that's a much less efficient procedure, but it's certainly workable. In any case, organizing is only part of a larger process, and it's time to move on.

Chapter Six

Writing

In the writing process, the first draft (the *writing* step in the POWER model) is not the final product. You are not expected to produce finished, polished copy at this point. It is only the middle stage of the POWER process of writing.

REASONS FOR WRITING A DRAFT

The first draft has four main purposes:

1. **To gather notes and ideas in one place.** In specifying the experience you'll draw on for your writing task (part of previewing), you may have stacks of notecards, piles of books with markers in them, photocopies of journal articles with highlighted paragraphs, and ideas dancing in your head. Chances are that some extraneous material is mixed in with it. In the writing stage, the information strewn over your desk comes together in a compact space, without the distraction of the irrelevant material.

2. **To make thoughts visible externally.** Thoughts are extremely malleable and easily changed. Your ideas may sometimes dance, jumble, fade, or even yell at you inside your head. When we write them down, we hold them to a fixed form, at least for long enough to decide if and how we want to change them. Writing them down is also a way of slowing the images in our heads, separating, sequencing and clarifying them.

3. **To add flesh to a skeleton outline.** A good outline or CPM chart or flow chart makes the structure of the developing document clear, but it's only a skeleton. When you write down the details, add the examples, and start filling in the transitions, your document begins to come alive.

4. **To provide concrete materials for polishing.** The first draft is only the raw material. But you have to have something external to yourself before you can evaluate objectively and polish effectively.

BLOCKS TO WRITING

When someone has a problem in the writing stage of the POWER process of writing, it's usually from one of four problems. First, failure to consider the whole communication context (previewing) can result in impossible situations, such as trying to satisfy two conflicting purposes or being unable to decide how much detail to include or what kind of vocabulary to use.

The second problem is lack of information. Not having something to say can certainly bring writing to a halt. Previewing includes gathering your information, and organizing should help you spot any places you need to fill in more information.

The third, and most common, problem stems from ignoring the *process* of writing and trying to create a perfect finished product in the first draft. Steve was a classic example.

"I've got the total picture," he said, "and I have no trouble getting organized. I do great outlines. But I just can't write."

"What happens when you try?" Dixie wanted to know. "What exactly do you do when it's time to write?"

Steve opened his mouth to answer, and nothing came out. He took a deep breath and pushed, but still nothing. "I don't know," he said. "Nothing. That's the problem." Quite clearly, Steve had himself tied in knots over the first draft.

Dixie placed a yellow pad on the table beside his outline and handed him a pen. "Show me," she said.

Steve picked up the pen and looked at the outline. He wrote a line, ripped out the page, and crumpled it. He tensed his jaw, wrote two whole lines, ripped out the page, and crumpled it. "It just doesn't sound right," he said, and he started again.

Dixie stopped him. "I see," she said. "You're trying to be perfect instantly, aren't you?"

When Dixie asked Steve to pay attention to what was happening inside his head, he discovered that he was listening to himself as if he were a critical member of his audience. This point of view could be very helpful to him as he evaluated his draft, but it stopped him cold at this stage. Dixie had him go back to his total picture and step into it, in his own shoes. Then he wrote, quite comfortably, as if he were simply talking to his audience.

The critical voice turns up frequently among our clients. Often it's a member of the intended audience, but sometimes it's a parent or a former teacher. These critics may have valuable contributions to make, but they must wait their turn. We usually suggest thanking the voice for its helpful intent, then asking it to wait until the evaluating stage of the writing process, when its suggestions can be properly appreciated.

Sometimes the critical voice is the writer's own. Buddy's first draft writing went very much like Steve's, but Buddy heard his own voice, chiding him for everything he wrote. He realized that this was the way he generally motivated himself in other areas: he'd tell himself he couldn't do it, and then he'd do it just to show himself he could. That strategy worked very well for most things, but it blocked him completely in this situation. He anchored a calmer, more business-like state of mind and suspended the critical voice while he simply talked on paper to his audience.

The fourth problem is a peculiar form of distraction and sidetracking. Writing generates ideas. That's what makes it such a good learning tool. Wonderful insights and new possibilities, sometimes about your present subject and sometimes about something totally different, can pop into your head while you're concentrating on writing that first draft. Your own creativity should be a delight, not a problem.

To take full advantage of your marvelous creative brain, write down its offerings. When the ideas are related to your current project, make notes to yourself in the appropriate place on your outline. Then you'll have them when you come, or go back, to that place in your writing.

Jot down notes about the other ideas, too, the ones obviously irrelevant to what you're working on now. You may want to remember them and use them later. Some people keep a special journal to catch stray ideas. Other people carry a pocket-sized notebook with them all the time. Others keep blank note cards handy in places they work. They collect the noted cards in a drawer or file box, and when they have a new project or want a fresh idea, they shuffle through the cards to see what inspirations may have turned up. Sid keeps a set of computer files for his ideas. Once you've made the note to yourself, you can let the thought go and turn your attention back to getting this first draft finished.

THE PHYSICAL FACTORS TO WRITING

Writing is a physical activity. To be sure, the brain had better be involved in the process, but by the first draft stage, if not before, certain physical constraints—paper and pen, word processor and its power, the limberness of your fingers, etc.—have to be taken into consideration. Here are some tips for efficiency:

Using Paper

If you are writing on paper (as compared to writing on the screen of a computer or word processor) by hand or by typing, consider these three practices:

- Write on one side of the page (the front) only.
- Skip lines or double space.
- Leave wide margins.

These habits make revising easier. With nothing hidden on the back, you can see the whole draft at once, and you can physically cut out chunks to eliminate them or splice them into a more appropriate place. The wide margins and space between lines allow you to cross out and write in alternatives and to splice in additions. If you feel guilty about wasting all that paper, don't. Save it and use the back for the first draft of your next writing task. Balance the small waste against the greater waste of both paper and your time in having to copy or re-type things unnecessarily.

Using Electronic Equipment

Composing electronically has two strong advantages over the pencil/paper method. First is the implication of process. That is, the words appear on a screen which continues to scroll up and out of sight. They can be called back and changed easily. There is no "hard copy" (printed version) to suggest finality. Second is the ease of change later in the revising stage and the speed of producing a second draft. A document can be revised without necessarily having to re-type the whole thing.

Most writers who compose with electronic equipment prefer to get a hard copy of an early draft so they can see all the parts in perspective. The advantage of the text scrolling up screen by screen can become a limitation when you want a good overview to evaluate what you've written. When you print the draft, double or triple space and leave wide margins, just as you would if composing by hand, so you'll have room to make revision notes.

While electronic composing seems to be overwhelmingly advantageous for complex documents, there are two disadvantages. One is dependency. Some people will postpone writing, even refusing to jot down those creative ideas that pop up while they're in meetings or waiting in lines, until they can get to their own computers. They don't want to have to copy it over. We're sympathetic with not wanting to rewrite or re-type unnecessarily, but we recommend catching all bright notions in a hand net—pencil and notepad—whenever they surface, so you'll have them when you need them.

The second disadvantage of electronic composing is that there is often no record of earlier drafts. For short reports, the final, polished version may be the only hard copy, fostering the illusion that the perfect document was done on a first draft. The writer knows better, of course, but inexperienced writers face frustration if they try to short-circuit the process here. Some writers save every draft, dating each file to keep track of the most current version. Others keep only a single back-up file and "save" their work frequently.

Using A Tape Recorder

A third way to handle the first draft is to talk it into a tape recorder. When a writer must do a lot of driving, has a member of the intended audience at hand ready to listen, or cannot manipulate pencil or keyboard, the tape recorder can catch the story. The writer, or someone else, can transcribe it later (one side of the page, double-spaced, wide margins) for evaluating and revising.

A few cautions apply to using a tape recorder for writing. The first consideration is the quality of your machine. If you're talking into it while you're sitting quietly at home or in your office, almost any kind will do. If, on the other hand, you'll be using it in your car, you need one that will pick up your voice clearly without restricting your hands and will not pick up too much road noise. Second is the quality of your speech. You'll need to speak a little more slowly and slightly more distinctly, especially if someone else will be doing your transcriptions. And finally, you'll need to be more alert in the polishing stage of the writing process for homophonic errors—words that sound alike but have different meanings.

A COMPELLING DRAFT

Remember the purposes of this stage of the writing process—to get your thoughts fleshed out, externally, in one place, so you'll have something to polish. You'll want to get on with this step as quickly as possible, so you can enjoy the rest of the process.

Begin where you have something to say, or where you're most interested. Your outline shows the logical progression of your argument, but you don't have to follow that sequence in producing the first draft. In fact, it's best not to begin at the very beginning with the introduction. You really don't have anything to introduce yet. Save the introduction and the conclusion until you've written something to introduce or conclude.

One primary rule governs this step in the POWER model: keep writing. Don't get bogged down in trying to find the perfect word or worrying about the use of a comma. Polishing comes in a later step. If you come to a hard section, skip it. You can leave room to fill in later, or you can write yourself a note at that spot for later development.

A sense of *compulsion* is an ideal state of mind for producing the first draft of a document. Most people have compulsions about something or other—being on time, flossing their teeth before bedtime, putting the top back on the toothpaste, etc. Analyzing that state of consciousness and anchoring it gives you a handy tool to compel yourself through writing this draft, or to get any other little chore done.

Steve was a compulsive picture straightener. He analyzed his state of mind when he sees a crooked frame on a wall—the vision in his head of the perfectly horizontal dotted line where the frame should be lined up, the particular set of muscular tensions in his stomach, tongue, and right arm reaching for the frame, the breathless quality of his own voice in his head saying "Get it!"— and anchored that state to the sight of his outline neatly lined up beside a yellow pad. Now, if you ask Steve what happens to him at this stage of the writing process, he still may not be able to tell you. But it's because, once he thinks about his outline lined up by his yellow pad, he can hardly stand to waste time talking about it. He wants to be writing.

GETTING THE RIGHT IMPULSE

This exercise will take you through the middle stage of the POWER process, writing that first draft. Remember its purpose. You're not expected to produce finished, polished copy. You only want to externalize your thoughts so that you can work with them more objectively.

Compelling Your First Draft

1.   Take care of your physical requirements first. Gather paper and pen, clear a space on your desk, or load your disk into your computer, etc. Choose a chair that will support you in a writing position. Writing is a physical activity. Your attention to creature comforts now will eliminate common distractions later. Put your notes on organization in a spot you can see easily, perhaps up on the wall in front of you. Have any content notes close by.

2.   The secret in the writing stage is to keep going while you get your ideas on paper. You need energy, perseverance, and excitement. So begin with establishing the right state of mind. Remember a time when you felt motivated, perhaps even compulsive, when you could hardly wait to forge ahead. It needn't be an important time, just an eager time. If you are one of those people who can't stand leaving a task unfinished, that feeling of having to get it done is the one you want here.

3.   Pay attention to the image in your head. In an associated state, see what you saw then, hear what you were hearing (externally and in your head), and feel those feelings.

4.   Use the worksheet as a guide while you enhance the image to make the feeling of motivation stronger, perhaps more exciting or more fun, too.

5.   You know you've got the right feeling if you look at your paper and pen and feel compelled to write. Anchor that state of mind. You may wish to create a general anchor for this state of mind, to use any time you want to motivate yourself. Or you may wish to make it specific to writing.

6.   To create an anchor specific to writing, imagine yourself writing that draft smoothly and easily, enjoying it, and moving right on through it without pausing. When the picture appeals to you, step into it (associate yourself with the image). If it's not comfortable, step back out of the picture and make whatever adjustments seem to be needed. When the picture is right, fire the anchor you established in step 5.

If you want to keep your general compulsion anchor separate from your writing compulsion, choose another anchoring place. Fire your step 5 anchor and, when the compulsive feeling is strong, create the new anchor, then proceed to associate that one with writing.

You may want to try a visual anchor instead of a kines-thetic one. Choose something you strongly associate with writing, like Steve's outline beside his yellow pad. It might be an object near your desk, or the desk itself, or a special writing implement. When you have the feeling you want in step 4, look directly at the object you've chosen. Repeat the process of getting the feeling and then looking at the object several times.

Some people like to have background music while they work. If that appeals to you, use it to create an auditory anchor. Repeat the exercise with your chosen music playing as you enjoy the state you want. Then you can play the music as an anchor to get you back into the state.

For a solid anchor, try combining the suggestions in this step. Make the mental image of yourself writing, add the feelings you anchored in step 5, and look directly at your chosen visual anchor as you listen to your music.

7.   Test your anchor. Walk away and think about something else. Come back, fire your anchor and write.

8.   Don't let yourself get side-tracked from your compulsion to finish that draft. When wiggling the fingers in writing stimulates new ideas and fresh bursts of creativity, make notes to yourself so you won't forget, but keep on writing. When the temptation to edit whispers in your ear, say thank you but no, thank you, not now. Only after this first draft is completed. If you get momentarily stuck, you can take a short break, or you can just skip that part for now. And keep on writing.

Chapter Seven

Evaluating And Revising

The last two steps in the POWER process are evaluating and revising. They are two separate procedures. Evaluating means weighing the worth of what you have written, deciding whether it's right, wrong, or OK but could be improved. Revising means re-seeing the communication situation now that the draft has actually entered into the context, looking again to see how the document needs to be changed to make the total picture more effective. In actual practice, the two procedures often happen so closely together as to seem almost one. In recognizing a flaw, you may perceive almost at the same time the way to fix it. The critic in your head may tell you exactly what you need to do to make your argument clearer—"Too flowery, just tell it to me straight," for example.

For effectiveness, good writers evaluate from at least two viewpoints, their own first, then their intended audience. They may also ask another editorial opinion, either real or imaginary. For efficiency, evaluating and revising should be done in a hierarchical order, content first, then structure and style. Only after you are completely satisfied with content, structure, and style do you consider things like typographical errors. Proofseeing the surface and checking for mechanical and grammatical errors are the very last of all. Because these processes are so interwoven, we treat them both in the same chapter. This chapter explains the hierarchy, illustrates the procedure, and offers two exercises to guide you through your own evaluating and revising.

THE EVALUATION/REVISION HIERARCHY

We begin with content first. After all, if the draft doesn't adequately convey the idea you intended, there's no point in polishing the prose. Worrying over where to put the comma before you've clarified the content may also be a waste of time if a later revision eliminates that sentence altogether. Once you're sure the idea is completely expressed, with all necessary information included, you look at the structure of your written document. Are all the related ideas in the same place? (Making a reader's outline of what you've actually written can help you here.) Is the sequence of ideas appropriate? Is each section of the document or each step in the sequence clearly identified? If your evaluation is unsatisfactory on any of these points, revise at this level before evaluating further.

When the content and its structure have your approval, move to the paragraph structure. Evaluate such things as topic sentences, length, transition, and coherence. Make revisions where you need to. Then review and revise sentence structure, word choice, and rhythm—the actual feel and sound of your words. Mechanics are checked last.

Having worked down the hierarchy with the substance of your argument, you next evaluate the layout, the signposts in the document that keep a reader on track, and the graphic support. Then you consider the overall impression the document will make, its physical appearance and its practicality in actual use.

Roger's Revisions

Ignoring this hierarchy of editorial elements gets many writers off track. Roger is a good example. His employer had high praise for the readability of his reports. They looked terrific, and they flowed smoothly. But sometimes they didn't quite cover the subject. She also complained about occasional sloppy editing— misspellings and punctuation problems—that interfered with reading.

In analyzing Roger's writing process, Dixie discovered that he began polishing his draft at the wrong end of the hierarchy. Roger usually checked grammar and punctuation first. "That's easy," he explained. "I do that first and get it out of the way." Then he spruced up his sentences and paragraphs. Of course, as he changed his sentences, he sometimes created an accidental grammar problem. But since he'd already checked grammar.... Once in a while, he'd get so caught up in the flow of paragraphs that he'd forget his original purpose. In his final version the step-by-step logic was flawless, but the path might lead someplace slightly different from his intended destination.

CHECK YOUR LIGHT BULB

Dixie asked Roger to change his strategy and begin by returning to his previewing picture and recalling his Self, Purpose, and Audience. Then he concentrated on the writer's side of the communication context. From this first position point of view, he evaluated the content of his draft to make sure what he'd written reflected the ideas he'd had in mind. Did the experience he'd selected as appropriate actually get included? Was it expressed so as to support the purpose? Was there a clear relationship between everything he'd written and what he had intended to accomplish?

The first task is to let the words on the page recreate the image. The first draft gets the ideas from the writer's head into words, externally. Now in evaluating, the process is reversed; read to see if the words will produce the images you intended. Are there enough concrete examples, sensory specific elements, to give detail to the picture? Are there enough abstractions to frame the picture or place it in context? In approaching his revision from this context, Roger could easily see where he'd veered off course. As he read the details this time, he consciously noticed the images they produced in his head. The overall patterns were missing. The details were clear, but the sequence of images didn't lead directly to his end goal.

The second task is to listen to the sound of the writing, hearing the words inside your head or out loud, as if you were talking to your reader. Roger enjoyed this part of the evaluation. When the sentences flowed and the tone was right, Roger's Self-image felt terrific. When the sounds jarred him, he was led right into the sentence-level revising he was so good at. But now, with his content picture stabilized, his revisions stayed on target.

CHECK YOUR READER'S WATTAGE

Of course, you want to be satisfied with what you write. But you also want your reader to be satisfied with it. In your Previewing, you identified your reader and your reader's purpose. The most effective writers give a great deal of attention to the reader's side of the communication model. The perfect message is perfect only if the reader can understand it—and understand it the way you intended. So once you're satisfied that what you've written matches your intention, you want to make sure the reader will get the idea you intended.

Professional writers of technical documents check the success of their work by field-testing their products with representatives of their audience. They ask them to read the document aloud and respond as they read by commenting aloud on any thoughts, questions, or feelings that occur as they read. You can evaluate your success on this score by imagining your reader actually reading your document and commenting out loud. As you watch and listen, do you like what you see and hear? Where do you want a different response? That's a spot you will target for revision. What else can you do to get the response you want? The answer to this question guides your changes.

The second procedure is to assume the reader's role yourself. Pretend you are the person who will read your writing. Imagine what it would be like to have your reader's attitudes, background, job, purposes, etc. Insofar as you can, assume your reader's physical characteristics: walk, general posture, facial expressions, etc. Now, read your document from your reader's viewpoint, noting your reactions.

Liz's Evaluator

Other viewpoints may also be helpful here. People with critical voices inside their heads put the nagging complainers to good use here. Some of the best general success stories from our workshops are of people who learned to make allies out of their critics. Liz is one example. She came to a workshop blocked at the organizing stage and at the writing stage by the memory of a grade-school teacher, who kept pointing out flaws in whatever she tried to write. Liz turned down the volume of the voice in her head so that she couldn't hear Mrs. James nag while she organized and wrote. But when she was ready to evaluate from the other side of the communication context, she turned the volume back up to a comfortable level and invited Mrs. James to attack her first draft. Several months later, Liz reported that not only was she getting helpful revision suggestions from Mrs. James, but that Mrs. James had had some good ideas about decorating her apartment and reforming her diet as well. A lighter Liz had found the POWER process spreading through her life.

POLISHING THE SURFACE

The very last step of evaluating and revising is Proofseeing. Now is the time, when you're sure your content and style fulfill your expectations, to check those surface factors, like spelling, grammar, and punctuation, that can destroy the reader's response. Don't underestimate their importance, for these are the first things a reader will notice if the errors interfere with reading. But don't let them get out of place in the process.

Considering the differences between the processes of reading and writing can put the hierarchy of Evaluating and Revising into perspective. The writer's concerns begin with generating an idea and getting it into words, then move to polishing the style of those words, and finally shift to presenting the material to the reader. A reader's impressions, however, begin at the other end. The diagram below, although it oversimplifies somewhat, illustrates the hierarchy of editorial elements in the order the writer is concerned with them and in the order they affect the reader's opinions.

Figure 7.1
Hierarchy Of Editorial Elements

Writer's Concerns

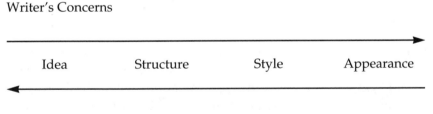

| Idea | Structure | Style | Appearance |

Reader's Concerns

This last step is traditionally called proofreading, or copyreading, and those terms emphasize the major problem in the task. When we read, we seldom see the details of a word. We see the general outline, and our knowledge of context fills in the detail. When we proofread our own writing, the problem is compounded; we see what we intended to write, not necessarily what is actually written.

In the individual conferences Dixie holds, when she asks clients about their understanding of grammatical or structural errors, they often say something like, "Why, I read right over that. And I read through this paper four times!" That's exactly what happens: people *read* over and through the writing on the paper to get at the ideas. In this final stage, you want to *see* what's actually there, not *read* what you intended to have written. Changing the term to proofseeing emphasizes the real nature of the task and helps program the brain to do it more effectively.

STEPPING INTO YOUR OWN WRITING

The next two exercises will help you evaluate and revise your own writing. They are presented sequentially. In practice, however, you will actually interrupt your evaluation to revise from your viewpoint of the communication context. That done, you'll return to evaluating from your reader's side of the picture, and then revise again.

Evaluating

Now is the time to invite the critics in your mind to voice their opinions, both positive and negative, about your writing. You'll begin with content and then work down to sentence structure and tone.

Evaluating Your Writing

1. Take the outline (list, flow chart, whatever) you made while Organizing and check each item with your written draft. Did you get in everything you intended? The actual order in which you treated each item may be different now, and that's fine. You're simply making sure you've included all the necessary information. Once that's done, you won't need that outline any more.

2. You began this project with an idea in mind, a purpose. With this idea firmly in mind now, go through your manuscript to see if what you wrote matches what you meant. Does it unfold in an orderly manner? Does it feel logical? As you hear what you wrote, what images do the words create in your mind? Do these images match your intent?

You may find places that aren't right. Make a note to yourself at that spot, so you'll remember what you need to repair. Unless it's something that can be fixed quickly, without losing your train of thought, leave it alone for now. Just note that something needs to be done, and keep on reading.

3. If you have major content repairs to make, such as complete restructuring (return to Organizing) or a large chunk of missing information to fill in (return to Previewing: Experience), do that now. If not, go on to step 4.

4. When you're sure the content matches your intention, check for compatibility with your Self. Get yourself firmly into the role you've chosen for this project. Remember those feelings of confidence and authority. Read your manuscript again, this time listening carefully to your own voice. Do you sound the way you want to? Is the rhythm appropriate? Comfortable? Did you maintain your role consistently?

There is, of course, a definite difference between the spoken and written word. But effective communication carries the sound of the human voice with it. Listening to your voice will pinpoint places you may want to make some stylistic changes. Some phrases may feel awkward. Some sentences may be too long, or too short. Generally, though, if you can say it comfortably, out loud, without losing your breath, your audience will be able to read it comfortably.

Again, as you read, make changes only if you can do so quickly, without losing your consciousness of your role. Otherwise, simply make notes to yourself about what the problems are as you continue through the manuscript.

5. If you have major changes to make here, after evaluating from your own point of view, proceed to the Revising part of the writing process. Then come back to Evaluating, step 6, to consider your audience point of view.

6. Once the content matches your intention and the general style is compatible with your role, you need to be sure that your audience will get the same concept and will respond as you wish. So call up your picture of your audience. Put

yourself in much the same position as when you were trying out Code. Now as you read through your manuscript, pay close attention to audience response.

Are there puzzled looks? Smiles and nods? Questions? Other comments? These responses give you clues for both content revision (more explanation, another example) and stylistic changes (more familiar vocabulary, less awkward metaphor). Make the changes you need if you can do so quickly, without losing your train of thought. Otherwise, just make notes to yourself.

7. If you have major changes to make when you've finished step 6, proceed to Revising, then come back to Evaluating, step 8.

8. Try now to read your manuscript as if you actually were your audience. As much as possible, put yourself in your reader's position, including posture and facial expression, if you can. Pay attention to your responses to what you read. Do you talk back to the writer? How do you feel? And especially, as you reach the end of your reading , what do you do?

You may want to make notes as you read, in case you have a chance to meet the author.

9. Back in your role as your Self, evaluate what you learned from your reader. Most importantly, did you accomplish your purpose? Did the reader's final response match your Previewing pictures of your purpose achieved?

If you're not satisfied with your reader's response, did you get clues along the way about changes that might help?

Gather your notes now, from all your Evaluating, and revise your manuscript.

Revising

Revising is essentially a re-seeing, looking at your manuscript with fresh eyes, from the perspectives you got as you evaluated. Most of the time, your evaluations show you not only where you need to revise, but also what you need to do.

Revising Your Writing

1.   Return to Previewing to see the context again from your new perspective. You may need to adjust some element of the total context. Perhaps you need a stronger Self, or a different Audience. Perhaps you need to revise your Purpose in some way, or alter your Code. In any case, your Experience now includes having written and evaluated the first draft of this document. Change, or verify, and strengthen your Previewing images.

2.   If your evaluation suggested some structural changes, go through the Organizing part of the writing process again. If not, go on to step 3.

3.   Pay attention first to the content changes you need to make. Return to the Writing phase of the writing process, this time using your Evaluation notes as a guide instead of your outline. As before, don't let your internal critics get you side-tracked into evaluating. With your Previewing image in your mind, let your motivated or compelled state of mind carry you straight through the content revision.

You don't need to rewrite, or re-copy the parts of your manuscript you're satisfied with. Just delete the stuff you don't want and add in the revised version.

4.   Go through the Writing step again, this time with your stylistic notes.

5.   If you've made substantial changes so far, go through the Evaluating process again, and repeat Revising steps 1-4 as needed.

6.   Turn your attention now to the physical manuscript. How does it look? Does the format attract rather than repel a reader? Can you improve its appearance (modify paragraph length, add headings, adjust spacing, etc.)?

If you've been handwriting your manuscript and done a lot of cutting and pasting of paper, it may look tattered and worn—downright repulsive from a reader's point of view. Ignore the physical reality for the moment and imagine how it will look when it's neatly typed. If you've been working electronically, this is a good place to get a hard copy, so you can spot spacing problems accurately.

7. Finally, check for surface errors in spelling, grammar, punctuation, etc. Be careful here to SEE what's actually on the page (or screen) rather than reading what you intended to write. Be sure to repeat this step after the typing is done. If you've been using a word processor, repeat this step with your hard copy, even if you've been using a spell-checker.

The Power POWER User's Guide in the appendix provides a good summary of the process of Evaluating and Revising. You may want to use it to keep your perspective on the interaction.

Congratulations! Your completed manuscript is ready for your reader, a POWERful piece of work. The easy, logical flow of the POWER process rapidly becomes a personal strategy. You may not even notice it, for as a POWER writer, your attention will be on the POWERful writing you are producing.

Part III

POWER Applications

Chapter Eight

POWER In Business Correspondence:
Writing For Immediate Influence

Most of us, when we were in school, had an English class on how to organize and write letters properly. In typing class we were shown how to set a letter up on the page to some standard form. But since we had no immediate use for these things, we promptly forgot them.

Forms can be re-learned quickly, but a more serious problem often hides beneath preoccupation with form: the problem of not knowing *why* you are writing to someone, once you are working in business. Many of us write letters because we think we're supposed to, rather than because we have a clear outcome in mind. Previewing, the POWER SPACE step, stresses the importance of having a clear self or role, a purpose, an intended audience, appropriate code, and adequate experience. These things are clearly very important in business letters, and there are ways to enhance them to get specific results. In addition, there are methods of organizing letters that can become standard forms for you and at the same time "sell" your ideas effectively. The same is true whether you are writing letters, memos, proposals, announcements, or any other kind of business correspondence. We'll take you through the POWER steps here to help you think specifically about your business writing. We'll give you an example or two of how it can be done and a checklist of important items to consider when you write for business purposes.

By the way, if you turned directly to this section to learn about writing for business, go back. You need to be familiar with the basic POWER model to make sense of, and get the most from, this chapter.

Previewing

Previewing your POWER SPACE is important for effectiveness and efficiency in all writing, but in business, where your writing means time and money, it's crucial.

Self

Who are you when you write for business? Well, you'd better be, at least in your own mind, someone the person you're writing to really wants to hear from, even if you've got bad news to deliver. You have something to offer that your reader really wants. As a corollary, having your offer accepted might improve your own life. These two facets of your Self foster your attitude of self-respect and reader-respect.

Whether you're offering someone an interest-free loan or desperately seeking any sort of employment, an attitude of self-respect in your correspondence is essential. If you don't respect yourself, why should anyone else? Generally speaking, nothing turns people off more than a begging or whining tone, or a sense of desperation. This is just as true in writing as it is in speaking. There are some business forms—minutes of a meeting, for example—where "respectfully submitted" and other self-depre-cating phrases are the norm. But that doesn't mean you have to think that way while you're writing or have this "one-down" attitude creep in anywhere else in your presentation. Our bias is to suggest that you never apologize for who you are, for why you are writing, or for asking someone to make a decision on your behalf. It's bad salesmanship and therefore bad business. Besides, once you begin with an apologetic tone, you'll need to play "catch-up" for the rest of your letter or proposal to make the sale. Don't put obstacles in your own path to success in writing, or in business.

You must also maintain an attitude of respect for your reader. After all, you should have enough self-respect that you only offer your services to others deserving of your respect. Granted, there are some people it's hard to respect, especially when they've behaved in a way that seems to you to be rude or stupid. You have little control of their stupidity, but you do have control of your own attitude, and you should have enough self-respect not to let yourself descend to their level. Moreover, if you want a positive response from them, you're more likely to get it if you offer a positive attitude.

In deciding who you are in your correspondence, remember always what it is that you want. As in all writing, your purpose will often dictate your role. You may, in fact, begin with what you want before you define who you are. A good strategy for this is to state clearly to yourself, in a sentence, what you want from the person or people you are writing to. Then ask yourself the question: "If I were they, who would I want to give this to, or do this for?" The answer to that question is, essentially, who you are in this correspondence.

Beyond that is the often asked question: "What are you really in the business of?" What goods or services do you provide and of what value are these to your customers or clients? If you don't have very clear answers to these types of questions, you are going to have trouble in business as well as in writing to others. Spend the time and effort to insure that you know who you are in your business, and why the people you write to should want to know you and work with you.

Purpose

Business writing is nearly always to get someone to do something. By its very nature this is so. It is amazing how often people forget this, but there is a reason. In our society it is not generally acceptable to be too presumptuous in dealing with other people. Most of us like to sort of "test the water" before jumping into some important relationship with another person. If we wait to see if that person will make the first move, then we don't usually feel as responsible for the outcome.

The problem with this is that if we want a specific outcome, and we don't take responsibility for it, we aren't likely to take the control to get it. In business this is a disastrous attitude. Effective salespeople have the outcome they want in the forefront of their minds all the time. They want the person they are communicating with to agree to something, usually to give them money for some goods or services. They ask for it, politely, but nevertheless clearly and directly. There is nothing wrong with this. In fact, it actually shows respect for themselves, their prospect or customer, and ultimately the business relationship that has been established.

At this point you may be saying to yourself, "But I'm not selling in my letters!" Yes, you are. You may not be asking for money for your goods or services, but you are definitely selling. Every time you write a letter, memo, proposal or any business communication, you are selling your ideas, your talents as a communicator, and the furthering of the business relationship with the person you are writing to. This is just as true within your own company or organization as with others. Accept it. Appreciate it. Enjoy it. Then develop the skill to do it well and practice it often.

In identifying your purpose, decide what it is that you are actually selling. Specifically, what do you want the reader to do when he or she puts down your letter or report? Buy something? Make a decision? Accept your proposal or idea? Change the way he or she deals with you? Take your advice or suggestions? Call you to talk about something? Write you back?

Again, keep in mind who you are in this context, the self or role you've defined. A clear image of yourself will help you in shaping what you write so that you are clearly the person who can make this "sale." There is an interesting argument that sales-people have been having for a long time in this respect. Some say that you simply have to sell yourself first, and that people will want your services or products, naturally, as a result. Others contend that you are better off thinking of yourself as a problem solver, someone meeting a need for the other person. In this sense you would sell them the solution to the problem, then convince them that you are the person who can supply that solution best (soonest, cheapest, neatest, etc.). This is probably one of those arguments without end. It really doesn't matter anyway. If you don't sell both, you'll lose. Sell both effectively, and you'll do business. The more you can meet someone's needs, and be a person they are truly happy to do business with, the better and longer you'll continue.

Though we have no intention of teaching you a great deal about sales here, a little bit can go a long way. We'll give you the most important aspects of sales so that you can incorporate them into your thinking and writing. It will make you a more influential person with those you do business with. If you are very experienced in sales, this can be a good way to incorporate more of what you know into your writing.

Audience

Business correspondence probably generates more fear than any other kind of writing, with the possible exception of school papers. In fact, it is probably the same fear. Do you sometimes have bad dreams at night about being back in school and out of control in some way? Perhaps missing a test, or showing up late for class, or not knowing how to get from one room to the other, or not being prepared in some way? Well, these are among the most common "out of control" dreams that people in modern cultures have! And there's a reason. Most people carry with them the thought of being graded on everything they write, even into their adult working life. In fact, they experience and act at work as they learned to do in school, for better or worse. They mentally replace the teacher with their boss, or the next person they need to write to. A real shame, because they carry with them the common and natural response to feeling out of control: fear of failure. That fear leads to an attitude of defensiveness, which is what makes so much of business writing stiff, boring, apologetic, or condescending.

Interestingly, defensiveness is very easy to overcome when you understand what produces it: imagining terrible things happening to you as a result of your actions, in this case your writing. As we've stressed throughout this entire book, unhelpful attitudes and emotions can be alleviated by following the POWER process guidelines. The operative mechanism here, as in all writing, is adequate planning to get the job done. That means you must know your audience as well as possible.

One advantage in business is that you often really do know the people you are writing to, or at least something about them. Otherwise you probably wouldn't be writing. Even if it is a form letter to a large audience, usually you have chosen which audience to write to by some logical method or perhaps carefully developed demographic information. You may, for example, have a mailing list of all people who share some interest, hobby, product, service, or need. Or you may write to a wide audience who all specialize in some sort of business dealing on a regular basis. Most often, though, you are writing to a person, or company, for something specific. We always recommend, if you do not have one, that you get a particular person to write to whenever you have the opportunity, rather than "To Whom It May Concern" or "Dear Sir or Madam." (Do you read further, when you get a Dear Sir letter?) Soften the "form letter" style, to personalize it as much as you can.

Another way to get to know the people you're writing to is to ask yourself at least as many questions about them as you did about yourself when defining your role. In business in the past few years it has become popular, because it has been found to be useful, to apply one of several personality style inventories to categorize employees or customers. These are used strictly for business purposes, meaning that the users have no particular interest in psychological makeup or problems. Rather, these tools are in use to help people understand the best ways to work with each other and to approach their customers. You don't usually have the opportunity to use these inventories on people you write to, but thinking about the possible variables involved—along with what you do know about this person, from previous contacts or the comments of others—can help you shape the information you want to present. You can even make some predictions about people you haven't had contact with if you know some information about them, but this is, of course, a bit risky.

The particular inventory we like to use comes, of course, from NLP and is called Sorting Styles. It is based on internal information processing categories called Meta-Programs. You don't need to understand how these really work to use them. They are simply tendencies we all have toward noticing different things, responding to them, and organizing our thinking and experience. These tendencies affect our motivation, decision making, and behavior toward others. Rather than describe them in detail, which isn't necessary, we'll simply ask you a number of questions about the person you're writing to, and you can either answer directly, or make your best assumptions, hopefully based on some good observations. If you really haven't any observations that can provide you with this information, cover as many bases as you can within each category, or set of questions. That way you'll be likely to hit your mark. This set of questions, by the way, is equally valid to ask about yourself. But remember, the answers change when you ask them in different areas of life and work. Keep the specific correspondence you need to make in clear focus while you think about the person you are about to write to.

NLP SORTING STYLES

Decision-Making Tendencies

Time What convinces this person of the value of something? Does your audience rely on what is in front of him, here and now, or does he need to see results over a *Time Period*? How long a time period would be necessary to convince him of the worth of your ideas? Is he more likely to pay attention to *Past* experiences, *Present* contacts and presentations, or the promise of *Future* services or guarantees? Would he need to see a certain *Number* of

Frequency successes, **Examples** or positive experiences, to make a judgment, perhaps independent of how much time it takes?

Sensory In making judgments, would your audience
Preference need to *See* results, or *Read* reports of effectiveness? Would she need to *Hear* from other people who have had experience with you or what you propose? Would she need her own *Experience*, say a trial run or sample of some sort? Does she have to "*Feel* it's right"? How about the five great questions: Who, What, Where, When, or How—to convince this person of what you propose? Depending on the answers to these questions, should you be writing at all? Would a phone call, meeting, demonstration or some other form of communication work better for you? Some combination? Should your letter simply be an invitation, or a request, for a meeting?

Motivation Tendencies

Action Is the person you are writing to more likely to
Orientation be *Proactive* or *Reactive*? In other words will he be likely, or even able, to act on his own initiative? Is he more likely to wait for something to happen, and then respond? Act, or react? In fact, the

most important question may be whether this person can act at all or must wait for someone else to make a decision, for any reason. Depending on the answer to that question, are you certain you are writing to the right person?

Source Does this person rely heavily on *External* information, that which comes from others to make decisions, or on what she feels and thinks based on *Internal* processes, gut reactions, clearly thought out procedures, etc.? How can you use this information to help both of you achieve your goals?

Direction Does this person tend to operate *Toward* pleasure, success and possibility, or *Away From* pain and perceived problems? In other words, does he respond to fear and punishment (sticks) or pleasure and rewards (carrots)? If you don't know, can you gracefully include both as possibilities in your correspondence? Can you show the negative consequences of not taking your advice or suggestions, while at the same time showing the advantages of following your lead? Will he respond to your presentation because of the *Possibilities* involved, or because he perceives he has no other choice, i.e., out of *Necessity*?

Comparison Style Will this person likely respond to how your products, services, ideas or proposals *Match* something she is already familiar with? Or, on the other hand, do you need to show how what you offer is a *Mismatch* for what is expected such as a unique feature of some sort? Does she look for things that are the *Same*, or things that are *Different*, when making a decision? If you don't know, can you include features of both sameness and difference in what you present?

Operational Tendencies

Scope It is possible to focus one's attention more to small details, or to more general, abstract ideas. Which should you concentrate on? Should you start with *General* ideas and move toward more *Specific* ones in your correspondence? Perhaps the other way around? Does this person have, or need to "see the big picture" to act on something, or a series of small details?

Priority   Can you list, in *Order of Priority*, the things relevant to your proposal that you think are most important to this person? How can you organize your thinking, or the content of your presentation, that will respect, appreciate, and respond to those priorities?

Rules   Finally, are there some *Rules* that this person chooses, or is forced to follow, in responding to you? How can you make it easy to follow these rules while responding favorably to you in the process?

Granted, as you looked over this list it may have seemed an overwhelming task just to answer a few of these questions. It may, in fact, not even be necessary in much of what you do. In some very important cases, however, thinking about these things will save you a great deal of time and also help insure that you have properly targeted your intended audience. If answering this list of questions seems like overkill to you, simply read it over and notice if any of the questions jog some memory or thought that might be of value. That is really what it is intended for. You might also, or as an alternative, look over the list during the Evaluating phase of your writing for the same purpose.

As in most writing, it is important to have a clear image of the individual or group you are writing to. Be able to see and talk with them in your mind to test what you have written. With the addition of the answers to the Sorting Styles questions, and a firm purpose in mind, you should be well on your way to producing convincing business correspondence.

Code

Most people who write business letters have some idea of what they think those letters are supposed to sound like. All too often they're stiff. Formal. Informational. Intellectual. Indirect. Uninteresting. Besides the fear and defensiveness we mentioned earlier, people may get this notion from some misguided ideas about people in business. The same sort of syndrome surrounds perceptions of teachers: they have no life outside the classroom;

they're packed away with the chalk at the end of the school day. It's understandable that little children associate teachers with a specific context. But adults frequently carry over that kind of limited thinking. It's almost as if business people—bankers, college presidents, lawyers, insurance adjusters, merchants—come packed in their offices to be activated promptly at 9:00 a.m. Often, the robots in the office encourage that kind of perception. The letters that come out of many offices could only have been written from one computer to another. Business writers seem to think that they and their correspondents must leave behind their desires, interests, beliefs, and tastes—along with the house, spouse, kids, mortgage, and personality. Forget this notion. The stiff, awkward language so often misused in business comes from losing sight of the real people in the context—you and your reader.

People remain who they are on the inside, no matter where they go. They still like the same foods, movies, colors, music, and *Writing* that they like in the privacy of their own den, bedroom, favorite easy chair, bathroom, or wherever else they do most of their reading. That's one of the reasons we asked you so many questions about who you imagine this person really is, on the inside. That's the person you are writing to, along with whatever facade may have been put up.

Intelligence and time are two of the most important and highly valued things most people have. Remembering this fact will help you balance courtesy and forthrightness in your correspondence. It is also likely to get you the same kind of highly valued treatment in response. In America, brevity and directness are a sign of respect for your readers' intelligence first, and the importance of their time second. In other cultures, brevity may need to be tempered, and directness may be considered rude. Again, know your audience.

Most people in business, however, prefer one-page letters. You can communicate a great deal in a page, both thoroughly and gracefully. Besides, most people don't want to spend too much time reading anything, especially if they are busy. And, as a general rule, the more successful people are, the busier they are.

There are, of course, times when one page simply won't do. If you must go to more than one page, make full use of layout techniques like headings to help your reader get all the way through your letter. If your information runs more than three pages, consider formatting it as a report. Then include a brief cover letter introducing the report and its importance for the reader. If there is some special set of details your reader needs, you could mention the page number in your letter. Many lengthy reports require an executive summary at the beginning. It usually highlights the ideas of most concern to the reader and provides a guide to the details in the body of the report.

Graphics are an important facet of business code. Whenever you have important information to present, and it is going to a very busy person, make full use of graphs, lists, charts, tables, and other visuals in addition to standard layout and design considerations to guide the person smoothly and comfortably through your presentation.

Experience

A modern truism in sales is that the salesperson must be client, or customer focused. That means finding out, first, what the client or customer really needs, or would like, and then finding a way to meet that need. A lousy salesperson will jump right in with suggestions or presentations of products or services with no regard for the customer at all. Good salespeople, on the other hand, select from their experience those parts that will suit their client. They take care to match what they have to offer with the client's need. Time spent assessing the person you're writing to, saves time in assessing your relevant experience.

Much of the time, when you write to someone, you may have the opportunity to ask him/her ahead of time enough questions to determine the specific needs. Then simply send a proposal, price list, set of possible alternatives or the like. During this information-gathering process you may also have picked up certain hints about what this person is really looking for that will help you decide which ideas to present. If you can briefly present the things you think would be most beneficial, you'll do better for yourself than if you have to give too broad an overview. More on this in the next section.

Organizing

Accepting the premise that all business correspondence is essentially a matter of sales, we then have an automatic pattern for organizing. In this kind of writing, the order in which you present your ideas, and how you do so, can be one of your most powerful communication tools for achieving what you want. All salespeople know that the order in which you gather information, or present ideas, is crucial. And the order in which you ask the person reading your letter to commit to something, make a decision, or take some other action, can mean the difference between success and failure.

Here we'll introduce you to, or if you are an experienced salesperson, remind you of, the "sales cycle." In client-centered selling the steps that the salesperson goes through are quite logical. The first step is finding or meeting a potential prospect for the goods or services. The second step is establishing a relationship based on some level of rapport and trust.

Next is determining the needs and interests of the buyer—gathering relevant information, and then choosing the products or services that match those needs and interests. The salesperson then presents the recommended product to the potential buyer in a way that clearly demonstrates the relationship between the features presented and the established needs of the customer. The presentation is usually followed by eliciting a clear acknowledgement from the customer that the product indeed meets these needs and interests, demonstrating to the salesperson that the customer understood and appreciated the presentation. Next comes a request that the customer make a purchase: the close.

At this point, there may be objections, hesitations, refusals, questions, and the like. These objections are re-phrased, explained, agreed to, or in some other way handled by the salesperson until the buyer is satisfied that the purchase is a wise decision. Then the salesperson closes the sale, collecting the money and delivering the product or service. Good salespeople will often make suggestions about how to use the product or service to maximize its effectiveness. They may even suggest what to do in the case of problems, so as to prevent "buyer's remorse," the buyer's feeling that the purchase was a mistake.

Finally a good salesperson will follow up to make sure the client is satisfied, sometime after the sale is completed. The very good salesperson will ask the buyer for referrals, names of friends or associates who might need or want the product or service. That's the sales cycle. This formula can be used, or adapted, to most letter writing in business, and certainly to proposals and other sales-oriented communications.

Contact And Rapport

As most salespeople will tell you, the most important thing throughout your contacts with another person is to maintain a high level of rapport. There have been many volumes written on how to establish rapport in sales. We highly recommend two NLP-based books that should be read by all business people: *Beyond Selling* by Dan S. Bagley III and Edward J. Reese, and *The Magic of Rapport* by Jerry Richardson.

Rapport is a state, or condition, of the relationship between people. It involves trust, interest, attention, understanding, and a special feeling of sharing. True, many people establish this state well with others almost automatically. But there are times when almost everyone will miss with somebody. We tolerate those times with people we know and love, but people seem less tolerant of breaches or interruptions in rapport in business contexts. For example, how many times do you need to have a bad meal, or be treated badly in a restaurant before you decide not to eat there any more? For about two out of three people we ask, the answer is the same: one. That isn't to say that recovery is impossible, but why make things more difficult than they need to be? The same can be the case in your writing. Understanding how this state develops and is maintained, especially in the context of business, can be useful to you in your writing as well as in the rest of your life.

Rapport needs to be monitored constantly during a business relationship. It also needs to be established fairly quickly, before the rigor mortis of disinterest sets in. So any techniques for establishing rapport need to be quick and simple, or they won't help much. The other side of the coin is that once we have achieved this state, the rapport will do much of our work for us. With great rapport almost anything is possible. Without it, not much is.

What work do we want the rapport to do for us? First, we want our audience to feel comfortable and at ease with us so that they will feel free to communicate openly. We want them to give us thorough and clear information on what they are interested in, what they need, and what we are likely to be able to do for them, whether now or later. Second, we want people to trust us. They must trust us to share their needs with us and to tell us about their problems and concerns. Then they must trust us to allow us to help them meet their needs and solve their problems. Third, rapport means understanding. We have all had the experience of getting confused in a conversation or accidentally confusing someone else. Then we discovered that we were talking on two different levels, or about two entirely different things without realizing it. With good rapport, this doesn't happen very often, and when it does, it can be quickly corrected.

In writing, this process of establishing and maintaining rapport starts with the physical appearance of your letter, neatly typed and appropriately laid out—you've done your part to make it easy for your audience to read it. You can't check this part until you've come to the end of the POWER process, of course, but you need to plan for it from the beginning. If you're using a letter style with a salutation, start with "Dear Somebody." Reach out with the reader's name or title to make personal contact. The opening lines often determine whether contact will be maintained or broken off immediately.

If you have had some previous, meaningful contact, you can immediately remind your reader of it. That does not mean formulas like this: "Per our conversation of 3 November last year..." or some other stiff, conventional phrase. No one wants to read that. Put the relationship in the conversation: "Our meeting Tuesday inspired me to experiment with a new contract style, and I'd like to work with you on it." Or, "I enjoyed talking with you about what we have to offer the other day, and I want to let you in on some new possibilities for us to help each other." This idea of working together and helping one another creates a feeling of teamwork and sharing that assumes the level of trust and rapport we think is important to have—especially if you're going to ask someone for something. Also, reminding the person of your last contact accomplishes two important things. First, it reminds the person, gracefully, who you are in case the conversation was some time ago. Second, it *fires off an anchor* for that person to go into the same state, with the same feelings about you, that he or she had in that previous contact.

If, however, the previous contact was not pleasant, or useful, you may want to introduce your letter with something to immediately change the person to a different state from that contact. For example: "I really appreciate the way you set me straight about your needs, and you'll be happy to know that we have made some big changes as a result of our talk." Thanking people for giving you a hard time can be a quick and easy way to turn a difficult situation around, since it acknowledges your ultimate respect for their opinion. It only works, however, if the respect is genuine and you actually follow through by making a change, or at least exploring alternatives. Doing your part to improve the situation will make it much easier to ask for something in return later. There is no right, or even best, way to patch things up with someone. Whatever approach you choose, the most important goal is to establish, or re-establish the relationship, before anything else. Sometimes a letter that does that one single thing only is best. Later you can follow up with a letter that asks for more.

If you have had no personal contact at all with the person you're writing to, you still want to begin with a friendly tone in introducing yourself. If your contact was suggested by someone with whom your audience already has an established relationship, it often helps to mention the name. The existing rapport between these two can "rub off" on you quite nicely. The mention of the name will act as an anchor for those feelings of trust the reader has with this other person. Just be sure you know what kind of relationship they really have. If you don't have the name of someone, you can still try to appeal to something you know the reader will be interested in. You may have an obvious point of mutual reference: "Your article on flatbed truck mounts was of immediate help to me in my business," for example. At the very least, there's some sort of connection between the two of you in your purpose for writing.

When the connection is tenuous, you may need help in strengthening your rapport with your audience. First, remember that rapport is based on something that is shared between people. This could be an opinion, a need, an interest, a problem, a profession, or even just being in business. It's how you present the sharing that makes it an effective tool. A good way to start is to list the things, ideas, needs and opinions that you believe you share with the person you are writing to. Then figure out a graceful way to point out this commonality, preferably as early as possible in your letter. Try phrases like, "We all need (believe, know, must deal with)..." or "You may share my interest in..." or "We can all agree that...." They may be overused, but they can be effective. Provided that you follow them with something that really does apply, they will help to create this feeling of sharing. The use of the words "we" or "us" or "share," will convey this sense of togetherness as well. As an exercise, practice coming up with rapport-building phrases that express the things you think you will share with most of the people you write to. Make a list. Then you won't have to think about them later.

Needs, Interests, And Presentation

Once you have established contact and moved to create rapport, you next want to invite the reader to be interested in what you have to offer. Appeal to the needs and interests you believe you've established. Remember, even though this isn't an in-person sales interview, the same order applies. You won't usually ask questions in your letter (unless information gathering is your intention), but you can remind the reader of the need. Then explain how your product, service, idea, or suggestion is an answer to that need.

Let's say you want simply to report to some colleagues or superiors about some research or information you've gathered. It can't hurt to remind them that they need it for something. Then when you give the data to them, they will feel that a need has been satisfied. A good sale. The same goes for presenting a suggestion or idea. First state the problem or reason for change, and then give your solution. State (or even create, if you must) the need; then fill it. Simple business.

Beyond that, though, creating interest is an art in and of itself. Interest is a state of mind as much as rapport, which means there are some subtle things you can do to enhance it in addition to concentrating on the things you already know the reader is interested in. Did you know that good salespeople are actually taught to create a sense of surprise, or even better, curiosity in their potential customers? The value is that this sense of curiosity gets people to focus their attention while you tell them exactly what you want them to know. Questions are one very good way to achieve this. Beginning a sentence with "Did you know..." accomplishes two things. First, it creates anticipation that the reader is about to learn something new. Second, it presupposes, in other words creates the assumption, that what you are about to say is absolutely true, even if it is only your opinion. Provided that you can back up what you have to say, in whatever form the reader needs to see or hear it, this is a very useful tool.

This sense of curiosity is a great way to build anticipation, which you then use to lead into what you have to offer. For example, "Did you know that 67% of people in your business say they need more...? And did you know that we provide the highest rated products of this type!" This approach creates interest, states a need you assume your reader has (67% say they do), and leads right in to presenting yourself or your company as the ones who can fill that important need. How about this to a co-worker that you need to develop solutions to a serious problem with: "Have you heard what the other departments are saying about our problem? I have an idea that just might straighten things out and convince them that we really do know what we're doing over here." This again creates a certain curiosity, and maybe apprehension, over a shared situation. Then it suggests that there is a solution that will not only get both parties out of trouble, but make them look good in the process! That's a way of using both the carrot and the stick we spoke of earlier, in two sentences.

Another way to get the attention of the reader is to use what salespeople often call "hot buttons." If you know of some special problem, idea, jargon phrase or even fad your reader is especially eager about, use it. For example, Sid does some management consulting in various kinds of businesses. He always makes sure that he is up to date on the latest trends that managers are looking for. This allows him to "speak the language" even if he doesn't really understand a lot about the details of a particular business. For example, phrases like "quality management," "team development," "effective communication," "management style," and hundreds of others are bantered about in business whenever there are problems. Since this is all the time, it is useful to know how to use them effectively and to find out which ones seem to mean the most to the people he talks with. These stock phrases are part of the broad business culture so it is important to Sid, as a member of that culture, to notice and share in their use—and to keep up with what's hot and what's not.

You can use those hot buttons as clues in audience analysis, too, of course. When Dixie hears someone refer to "dolphin strategy," she makes structural adjustments in her workshop format to take advantage of more cooperative learning activities. She finds differences in format and tone preferences between corporations with strong chains of command and those with organizational charts emphasizing quality circles. She uses their language to explain the concepts she's demonstrating. Awareness of certain hot buttons influences the code she chooses and the way she connects what she's offering to their needs.

Sharing the use of hot buttons creates rapport. When you see people's eyes light up, hear their voices crackle in some distinctive way, or notice in a letter that some tell-tale term creeps in about every twelve to fourteen words—those are hot buttons. By all means, push the appropriate button, at least a little, when making a proposal. Your consideration of your audience in using their language invites rapport, interest, and motivation all at the same time.

Closing And Moving Forward

As we said earlier, the sale ends with a close, handling any objections to the sale, taking care of buyers remorse (in advance), and moving on, perhaps asking for more business or referrals to others. Can you do these things in your letters, memos, and proposals? You bet.

To begin the process, ask for what you want. You may briefly summarize your presentation first, but make sure you get to the point. "I'd like you to call me so we can set up a meeting to discuss implementing this new program" is much better than "I hope you'll give this your careful consideration." How will you know if you get any consideration at all, careful or otherwise? Ask for a response, clearly. If it's a sale, "Please fill out the order form and send it to me along with your check." This is a lot surer than, "Thank you for the opportunity to present my products to you. I sure hope you'll take some time to think about them for a while."

An important note to the squeamish. We used to watch people wring their hands, and listen to lots more moaning than we were interested in, about how to ask for money. Some people will go to great lengths to avoid any mention of money changing hands so as not to offend the reader. *Not* mentioning money usually offends the reader, who must continue wondering not only how much, but how to find out how much. People in business expect to pay for things that are worth having. If your products or services are worth having, state the price clearly and proudly, without subterfuge or apology. Period.

You may also choose to anticipate problems with or objections to what you have offered in your letter. Lawyers will often tell you that one of the smartest ways to handle weaknesses in your case is to point them out yourself, first, before the other person gets the chance. This technique can accomplish four things. First, it throws people off guard a bit—another surprise—which gets their attention and their curiosity engaged. Second, it communicates that you are looking out for their best interests by showing the pitfalls in your proposal. Third, it allows you to answer the objection before it damages the rapport or your credibility. Finally, it actually strengthens your case by demonstrating that you noticed the problem but didn't think it was important enough to prevent the ultimate acceptance of your ideas.

The final thing we like to finish our letters with is a positive statement that carries the relationship into the future. This can be something as simple as, "I'm looking forward to a great working relationship with you" or "I'll call you next week when I'm in your area." We're looking forward to hearing from you how this organization pattern has increased the effectiveness of your letters.

You may be thinking that the details of the sales cycle conflict with our earlier suggestions about brevity. All of what we have described above can be done in two or three short paragraphs. In NLP we have a word for an economical display of skill and artistry: elegance.

WRITING

One of the advantages to business writing is that you will probably write many things that are similar, over and over again. Instead of boring yourself, you can increase your efficiency. As we suggested in the section on establishing rapport, you can practice stock phrases that achieve your usual goals with your usual readers. Then you can save them and use them over and over again with lots of different readers. Keep a folder or computer file of good phrases, sentences, and paragraphs, of sample letters that do what you need to do, and of standard things you use in your letters and reports. With the aid of computers, which most businesses use routinely now, this "boiler-plating" becomes even easier. These resources then become a regular part of the Experience step in the POWER model. Simply go through what you already have done and steal it from yourself. This, too, is legal.

Beyond boiler-plating, the writing phase should be the same as in other kinds of writing. Quick and easy. It will be cleaned up and enhanced when you evaluate.

EVALUATING AND REVISING

As in all writing, begin by making sure that you have accomplished your purpose. Check the concept level first, both from your point of view and from your reader's. Then check the structural level. Check grammatical and mechanical details last. Revise at each level before evaluating at the next.

Finally, make sure this piece of writing looks good, visually. One common and useful trick is to set it on something, a table or mantel, across the room from you so that you can see it, but not read it. Does it look good from a distance? You should have an aesthetic "balance" between words and white space so that it doesn't look too cluttered or dense. A lopsided or cluttered-looking letter can make the reader feel lopsided and cluttered— no matter how good the writing. This response is especially true in highly visually oriented people, but remember that writing invokes the visual sense anyway. Also ask yourself, "Does this look 'professional' in whatever way it needs to so that it shows respect for me, my proposals, and my reader?" This is more than making sure the grammar and spelling are correct, though those things are certainly very important. All of these visual components come into play when someone reads any business correspondence. At least on an unconscious level, the reader may actually judge your business competence by the competence of your communication. This may be totally unfair, but much of what is unconscious is. You can use it or be used by it. Take the time necessary to demonstrate your care and competence in every way possible.

Here's a checklist to help you evaluate your writing more specifically from a business angle.

Content
Your Side
- Does what you wrote accurately match your intentions?
- Does it portray an appropriate image of you?

Your Reader's Side
- Will the reader interpret what you wrote the way you wish?
- Does the reader have all the information necessary to take action?

Sales Cycle Structure
Contact and Rapport
- How have you established the connection between yourself and your reader?

Needs and Presentation
- Have you shown how your offer or request meets your reader's need or interest?

Close and Movement Forward
- Have you specifically asked for what you want?
- Have you laid the ground for future action?
- Have you anticipated and appropriately handled objections?

Sorting Styles
Decision-Making Tendencies
- Have you placed the need and solution in appropriate time—past, present, or future?
- Have you given enough examples?
- Have you engaged the reader's senses? Have you put the reader in *touch* with the good things you both will be *hearing* as a result of all you've *shown* in your presentation?

Motivation Tendencies
- Has appropriate action (proaction or reaction) been suggested?
- Has the appropriate source for decision been solicited?
- Has an appropriate direction for movement been suggested?
- Have appropriate comparisons been made?

Operational Tendencies
- Has an appropriate level and sequence of specificity or generality been used?
- Have priorities been suggested effectively?
- Have appropriate rules been acknowledged or invoked?

Visual Impact
Graphic Support
- Have appropriate graphic aids been included?
- Does the layout and design support the document's intentions?
- Is it "user friendly"?

Proofseeing
- Is the copy free of all mechanical and grammatical errors?
- Does the document look inviting?

When you have gone through all of those steps, ask yourself the most important question: "If I were the person I'm writing to, would I do what I've just been asked to do?" If the answer is *not* yes, you are *not* finished. Simple.

Chapter Nine

POWER In Literary Writing

Literary writing (sometimes called creative writing) poses some special considerations, but the POWER Process works for fiction and poetry, too. Since this book is not meant to be a complete guide to literary writing, we'll assume that you have some knowledge of fiction, poetry, or drama and how they are constructed. We simply want to show you how to adapt the POWER Process if literary writing is your interest. Let's go through it again, and at each step take a closer look at, and listen to, each of the processes.

FICTION WRITING

Many writers of fiction will tell you they write strictly for themselves. They have no interest in pleasing any particular audience. Also, they will say that their characters determine the organization, action, dialog, and other significant features of their stories. The actual writing process, for many of them, is long, arduous, and often lacks a clear direction. These writers will, in fact, not always know how the stories will end, and have to wait until they get to the ending to find out themselves!

If that seems very unlike the POWER model we have been describing for you, don't be too quick to judge. Even writers of fiction need to go through many of the same processes as those we have described. Perhaps in a different order. Often with different approaches. Certainly with different criteria for some of the steps in the process. The POWER Process, however, even as we have described it thus far, is quite useful and adaptable to writing fiction.

Previewing
Self

The first step is, of course, Previewing. Begin by determining your self, your role; who are you, the author, really? In fiction the role of the writer is usually determined by vantage point. You can be an omniscient observer, a narrator, or even one of your characters. In some cases, you may switch roles for effect. The same kinds of Previewing decisions need to be made here, but for different reasons.

In creating effective fiction, the point of view determines how the reader will see and hear the action, and then what feelings will develop from this. Often writers will try different points of view to discover which best suits their purposes. For example, to create an intellectual experience, somewhat devoid of emotional or truly visceral feelings, the writer may take the point of view of a dispassionate observer, also devoid of these feelings. In contrast, an omniscient observer may know the thoughts and feelings of all the characters, and convey them clearly. On the other hand, a limited omniscient observer may choose to share only those thoughts and feelings that will create a certain kind of understanding on the part of the reader. From the point of view of one of the characters, the author can give all the thoughts and feelings of that character, but not of the others. This viewpoint would limit the reader's knowledge of the thoughts and feelings of other characters to what could be observed and discerned from their actions, accurate or not. The reader's sympathy, then, is likely to be with the narrating character, as opposed to others. Again, these are only examples and generalizations. Literature is known as much for its exceptions to rules and guidelines, as for anything else.

Even in fiction, you must have a clear point of view throughout your work. It may change, but that change must be deliberate on your part. You might ask yourself, "Who do I think I am, to be writing this?" You can ask that question a number of times, in different ways, and come up with some very interesting insights. That question also leads us to the next step, Purpose.

Purpose

Why are you writing this? What goal, outcome or response do you want from your reader? You may be trying to create a particular intellectual or emotional experience. Perhaps you want to convey certain ideas or opinions, just as in non-fiction. Perhaps the story is meant to be a great metaphor about some particular or general human experience, to teach some lesson or system of thought. Your purpose could, however, be simply to tell a good, entertaining story, a worthwhile purpose in itself.

The purposes for writing fiction are as varied and personal to the author as they are in all other writing. Your text is built around your intentions in fiction just as in non-fiction. Often, though, the writer of fiction can be vague enough to allow the reader to reach whatever conclusions he or she wishes, certainly as worthy an outcome as any other.

If you're uncertain about your purpose, pay close attention to the fiction you most like to read and decide what it does for you, or in you. Do you learn from it? Does it make you feel something special? Does it, on the other hand, take you away from your feelings in some way that is valuable to you? How have you changed or grown as a person from what you read? How about those around you? We both like science fiction but for different reasons. Dixie likes to escape in science fiction/fantasy tales and to explore generally untapped human potential. She usually brings back some of the heroine/hero's strengths and talents to help her cope with "regular life." Sid likes the sociological and political explorations you can do in a far-removed setting. He also likes short stories so he can squeeze them between other commitments. Dixie prefers novel-length fiction; when she's met a character or concept she likes, she wants time to push the development further and to enjoy their company. If you can duplicate in others the most valuable or cherished results you get from reading, then you'll have done something worthwhile. If you clearly understand, as much as this is possible, how to get these results, your job will be easier.

Audience

We already mentioned that many great authors swear they have no audience in mind when they write. Most will say they write to please themselves. To us, this is as it should be. Good writers are also good readers. They know what good writing is, and they have high standards of both quality and style. Good writers are also passionate about what they write. They care mightily about their characters and plots (their grant proposals and poems, too), and this passion comes through as quality writing. Some will say that passion is the most important trait of a good writer, one that separates good writers from bad ones.

In addition, experienced writers may know very well what they can sell. That means they are writing for editors who buy, in part, and the public who buys as well. But experienced authors, marketing to the general public, whoever that is, almost never consider that to be the audience, for the same reasons we've suggested you shouldn't. General Public is impossible to please. Some will like a work, some won't. Now, individual editors are something else. They have faces, voices, likes, and dislikes that can help in Previewing.

Authors do want readers, however. When they write to please themselves, they also write to please others like themselves, people who have similar tastes in reading. Since they know their own tastes well, they often delay bringing audience into consideration consciously until the Evaluation part of the writing process. Authors can decide what kind of audience to write for ahead of time and shape the story to please those readers. Or authors can let the story shape itself and then decide what audience might be an appropriate market for the story.

In general, what we are saying is that experience can teach writers what and how to write, just as it teaches all of us how to choose what to read. Good, experienced authors have trained minds, even though much of the training may have been unconscious. Training the unconscious mind is what this book is about.

Audience And Character Development

Does all this mean we should scrap the Audience step, once we become experienced? Not necessarily. In fiction, we can use it for something else, in the same way it was designed. The good writer of fiction will spend the time on developing the personalities of characters that the writer of non-fiction uses in determining the needs of the audience. All of the exercises we described for clearly imagining and talking with the external, reading audience are applicable here. A good story teller will imagine the characters as if they were alive and real. Each character will have a look, a voice, emotions, and individual traits and mannerisms. The more thoroughly the author imagines these qualities, the easier the character is to describe. More importantly, perhaps, vivid characterization will determine how each character responds to other characters, to the setting in which the story unfolds, and to the action and situations the plot offers. The other characters, then, become the internal audience for the story.

Many people who teach fiction writing suggest that careful character sketches are the key to realism. They insist that these descriptions be thoroughly written out before any of the actual writing is done. This advice is similar to our suggestion that you be sure your audience is clear, with whatever notes you need close at hand. Also, the Designer State Worksheets can be used for character development as well as in determining the needs of an audience. Many authors imagine actually playing the role of each character in a story—becoming that character for a time. That way they get to know them more intimately, as well as testing out individual responses and actions. The worksheets can serve as an additional tool in this process. You can develop a worksheet for each character you play, and anchor that character's role. This is actually the process that actors use in "getting into character" though it is often an unconscious process for them, just as it often is for an author.

Even in initially developing the characters, the same process can be useful. Good writers will tell you that their characters often come from their lives, from people they know, or have seen or heard. It is easy to imagine you are playing the role of someone you know well. It's a bit more difficult with someone you don't know so well, but still possible. Often writers will do a "composite" of several people to make up a character. They simply imagine how someone has behaved in a certain situation and combine it with the ways others have behaved. Then it is a matter of making sure the behavior can be realistically consistent for that character.

Sound familiar? Think back to the section on making sure your audience is consistent and deciding how to resolve conflicts, and you will have the same processes available in deciding about consistent characters. Try your characters out in a variety of situations, just as you earlier imagined trying out different kinds of information on each of your audience members. This is largely the same task, so it involves the same decision-making skills.

One important difference in Audience needs to be clearly stated here. If you have conflicts between audience members when writing non-fiction, you may have to resolve them. In fiction, however, these conflicts between your characters can be the compelling features of the story. Explore them thoroughly, and your characters will truly come to life for you. Let them fight out their conflicts, and they may tell you their story while you write it down.

Another interesting narrative technique is that of having a character step out of his or her role to talk directly to the audience in a soliloquy or audience aside. Shakespeare used it effectively, and it still works today, in movies and television as well as novels and stories. The soliloquy can make an interesting test for a character, while developing the character and the story, even if it isn't used in the final version. The same goes for all of the foregoing character development methods. You will find, if you use these ideas, that you may do lots of writing before the actual Writing stage has begun.

In the chapter on writing business correspondence we introduced you to the concept of Meta-Program sorting patterns. These are the tendencies that people engage in such as moving **Toward** pleasure or **Away From** pain, orienting themselves to the **Past, Present,** or **Future** and so on. Take another look at that section for some really interesting character traits you can use. Why not do a thorough personality inventory of each of your main characters? Those questions we use to evaluate our potential customers in making a sale, are just as valid in creating compelling characters in our stories. Try it out. You'll surprise and delight yourself with how much you can learn.

So, basically, this step in our model, Audience, is replaced by careful attention to the development of characters. All of the same provisos apply. In fiction you mentally "work" the characters against each other, whereas in non-fiction you would try the material out on an audience. You simply let the characters try their material out on each other and on the setting you have created for them. Then imagine them, as well, playing out their newly created lives in front of an imaginary audience. And have fun!

Code

What about Code? Well, the fiction writer's Code will be determined by the Self, or point of view, and the characters. So, of course, the author will develop different codes (style, colloquialisms, dialects, slang, and so on) for each character, however it's most appropriate. Just as in other kinds of writing, each code needs to be tested to be sure it works effectively. This is often the most difficult part in writing fiction well. Believable dialogue is developed by constantly playing it back and listening carefully, just as you did earlier in trying out jargon and other language on your audience. There is no substitute for using your imagination—and a good, well-trained (practiced) ear.

A good exercise is to spend time listening to people who talk like your characters. In fact, listening closely to how all people talk is wonderful training for life, as well as writing. Write down interesting phrases you hear from people. Then carefully, systematically, make small changes in these phrases and find out what the effects are. Ask yourself some probing questions about these people, as they speak, in your mind and on your paper, in new ways. Does the rhythm of their voice change? Does the meaning, or their intent change? Do these subtle changes seem to change the very nature of the person speaking? Would the speaker have to have a different background, attitude, or setting to make changes like the ones you've tried? What can you learn about people from how they use language? How can you convey these learnings through your own use of language?

Experience

The Experience step is just as important here as in any writing. You as an author need to know enough, and have enough background, to make your work readable, believable (if that is important), and rich. You need to know about people and their behavior, settings, and whatever else makes up the world you create, no matter how artificial it may actually be. Many experienced writers will tell you that all writing is about people, no matter what kind of fantasy world, or fantasy creatures, the story may be about. This is because, as people, we simply project ourselves, our experiences, our prejudices, and our limitations into everything we write. All of our writing is, ultimately, a reflection of who we are and what we know and experience. For our writing to grow, we need to do the same.

Careful development and good decision making are the keys to good fiction just as they are to good non-fiction. You need a basic understanding of the processes and skills of compelling storytelling, of course. Then attention to point of view, purpose, characterization, language, and experience will lead you past the textbook plot patterns and exercises to your own good writing.

Organizing

Many people ask, at this point: "Don't you have to know what your characters are going to do, and where they are going to go, before you can even find out how they will behave?" Like an outline (remember that's now a generic term for any visual representation of the relationships of your ideas) for non-fiction writing, a plot outline always helps, and it rarely works out exactly. Most writers do begin with some sort of plot outline, some of them quite detailed.

However, as we mentioned earlier, many great writers of fiction will begin writing with only a vague notion of where they are going. Even when an author has a fairly complete idea of the story line, or plot structure, he or she may often make major changes as the story goes along. Characters must be allowed some leeway to shape their own story, based on how they would realistically act and respond to one another and the environment. Authors often speak of their characters taking on a life of their own, regardless of the author's intention. It may be that the more interesting and compelling the character, the more this is so.

That is not to say a good writer does not organize. Many of these writers take the alternative process of Previewing, Writing, and then Organizing. They prefer to allow the characters to develop and then see which ones will be most interesting. Sometimes a minor character takes over a story. Or several plot lines develop, and the author must decide whether to try to weave them all together or to choose one for development and save the others for the next books.

For those select few who seem to simply sit down and let the story write itself, we speculate that on an unconscious level, there is a more solid and clear organizational pattern than on a conscious level. Our contention, however, is that skilled writers of fiction have trained themselves, on an unconscious level, much better than the rest of us. So they are more apt to be able to predict a satisfying outcome to their writing.

It is also probable, that since they have carefully designed their characters, the words and actions of the characters control the plot. Interesting characters make a story interesting. Their responses are usually what makes a story work.

Lastly, there are probably a limited number of organizational, or plot, forms and patterns that will work. Even what seems random, or chaotic, to us has some underlying logic and form. It may remain unconscious to us, or even to the author, but that doesn't make it less real (and it provides endless fodder for scholarly papers and dissertations). The form and logic of the unconscious is just as real and unavoidable as that of the conscious mind; it is simply less obvious. "Stream of consciousness" usually more literally means the stream of someone's unconscious: the author's. In many cases, as readers, this apparent lack of form forces us to pay closer attention to the characters and the action. This can pull us, powerfully, into the experience the author intended. Isn't that what reading fiction is all about anyway?

Writing

How about the Writing step itself? As far as we can tell, it's only slightly different from the writing of non-fiction. It is still important to get as much down on paper, as quickly, and as thoroughly as possible. One difference, which may be an advantage to the fiction writer, is that if your characters do something that is inconsistent with who they are and how they should behave—"out of character," in other words—it will be immediately noticeable (provided, of course, that the characters are developed well enough to begin with). In that case, you can take the time to change it, especially since it can so heavily impact what follows in the story. Also, you may need to check your dialogue and action frequently with your Preview to make sure it stays at least reasonably close to the mood you are trying to create. Generally, though, keep the compulsion to keep writing. All inconsistencies can be repaired in the Evaluation step.

This interplay between conscious and unconscious processing during the writing phase is both helpful and interruptive. You may realize that the characters are not quite developed enough, and you may have to go back to more thorough development, or even revision, before finishing your first draft. More often, though, you may discover that the characters are taking their own turns, setting their own directions, simply because of who they are and how they are reacting to one another and the circumstances. As we've said, interesting characters often dictate their own circumstances, rather than just responding to them, just as interesting people do. They really do seem to have a mind of their own. In reality, of course, it is the (unconscious) mind of the author. A good author, again, has a highly trained unconscious.

Evaluating And Revising

Once you have a draft, the Evaluating and Revising steps in the process are pretty much the same as in non-fiction writing. The major difference, of course, is that the criteria for success and effectiveness are different. But these were still determined in the earlier steps, so the main question to be asked in this step of the process is unchanged: does the writing convey what was intended?

Additional questions to ask at this point involve how well each character has maintained his or her individual integrity as a distinct person. Was each character consistent in both language and behavior? If not, was there a believable and necessary reason, within the story itself, for these changes or inconsistencies? Is the overall story believable? Does it matter if it isn't? As a reader, can you understand the motivations, desires and conflicts of each character? Do they remind you of people you know or can at least relate to? Can you feel sympathetic toward at least somebody in this story—as a reader?

Also, does the story have some other message within it, outside of the characters themselves? Is it metaphorical to something else that is worth knowing about? Should this relationship be obvious, or remain unconscious to the reader? How did you do on this count?

How does the story sound—literally? Writers often mention reading their work-in-progress aloud to someone. Are the rhythm and length of the sentences comfortable? Effectively uncomfortable, if that's what you intend? Then what do you see as you "read through" the words to the scenes you're depicting? Are the descriptions rich enough? Do they invoke all of the senses so that the reader can get caught up in the scene with the characters? Does the dialog help the story? Does it tell us about who the characters are in some special way? Does the language convey something about you, the author, that you want to convey to your readers?

Since language is such an auditory feature, we'd like to suggest another exercise for you to try out and have some fun with during the Evaluation phase. Pick a piece of description or dialog from your writing. Then pick some music that sets the mood you're trying to create with that written piece. Now play the music and read the piece, out loud, at the same time. You don't have to have the rhythm down perfectly, and don't sing it— just read. Simply test the writing for mood and tone, with the music as a sort of guide to measure against. This may help you to create more evocative sensual writing. Musicians and other artists can teach writers something about creating powerful experiences. Bring all of the senses to bear in as many ways as you can, and learn from the experience.

Writing fiction can be more challenging, and therefore more fun and interesting, than writing non-fiction. (Dixie would argue that nothing could be more challenging than some of the multiple audiences she's had in industry or more fun than some of the stories behind the technical reports. Sid's unconvinced.) We think that the POWER model, and all of the NLP skills built into it, can be applied to great advantage in story telling. Anything that helps a writer develop ideas and fantasies in a compelling fashion, train the unconscious mind, and move systematically, and passionately, through a project, can only add more good writing to all our lives.

DRAMA

Playwrights face the same constraints that fiction writers do, plus a few more. Two occur in the Previewing stage of the writing process. The first difference is **Self**, or point of view. As a dramatist, your options are limited. You can't tell the audience what your characters feel and think. You can give only a few stage directions to indicate interaction of the characters. They're on their own, and if you want your audience to understand what motivates a character, the character will have to reveal it directly. You'll need to assume the role of the character more immediately to discover what actions, what words, will demonstrate the underlying emotions. The other characters are the internal audience for the character you're concentrating on, just as they are in fiction. As you assume each role in turn, notice how the other characters react, just as you would when you imagine presenting your technical report to your primary reader.

Audience is definitely different in drama. In fiction, you're writing for readers. In a play, your primary audience will be watching and listening. A reader can look back on the page, whereas a theater audience has only one chance to hear each line. Of course, with the tips you practice from this book, your play will soon be a major motion picture, then the monthly choice for all the video clubs, and then your audience can rewind and catch the line again. Meanwhile, however, build in enough redundancy to make sure a listening audience can follow. For details crucial to the plot, either give them a dramatic build-up to focus attention or have them repeated a few times.

Evaluating a play must be more visual than any other kind of writing (except perhaps, descriptions of a technical process). As you read your script, see the characters in your mind as they will appear on stage. Watch them as they move and speak. Is the action physically possible, given your setting? If you're thinking screen-play, you have more leeway with physical laws, but you must consider the physical logistics of your setting and the action in it.

POETRY

Poetry imposes tighter restrictions than any other genre, so of course there are some special adaptations in the POWER model, primarily in the Previewing stage. This section assumes you have some familiarity with the mechanics of constructing poetry and simply want to do it more effectively. If you know what you like but don't know anything about how it was crafted, you might want to start with a good book on the basics of prosody (poetry-making). The Bibliography makes some suggestions. Then use this book to complement their advice.

Previewing
Purpose

This time, instead of beginning with Self, begin with Purpose. If your purpose is narrative, you have the same considerations the fiction writer does. Once those decisions are made, you have the additional constraint on your code of the verse form you choose. If your purpose is to evoke a mood, capture an image, or stimulate a new perception, you may still use narrative as your vehicle, but you may choose a lyric form. If that is your choice, you now consider your role as poet.

Self

How do you see yourself as a poet? Is your self-image the same as the one you see in the mirror each morning, or are you charged with holy insight, proclaiming from the mount, with robes flying in the wind? As an experiment, try expressing your idea from several different roles. Imagine the costume, setting, and stance for each persona. The wise woman next door sounds considerably different from the Parnassian priest, doesn't she? The psychic seer has another kind of voice.

When professional poets read their own work, they often comment about the poem, how it was written, what the intent was, what technical problems were presented, and so forth. What difference do you notice between the voice making the commentary and the voice reading the poem? For some poets, the only differences are the ones between extemporaneous speaking and reading a manuscript—very few differences for a good speaker and good reader. For others, however, it's as if another person has stepped to the microphone: tone quality, cadence, posture, and bearing all change. Which voices do you like best? Try those on, too, and see which ones you like for yourself. Poets don't all sound alike, and you don't have to sound like somebody's preconceived notion of "Poet" to write good poetry.

Your best poetry will have your own voice. Your poet voice may be radically different from your voice as an engineer or manicurist, but it doesn't have to be. It may change, too, depending on your purpose and your subject matter. Most poets find a favorite poet Self, but they vary it to suit changing material. Your poet's voice does, however, have to be authentically yours, in the Self you choose.

Code

Self and purpose naturally influence code. In the case of poetry, vocabulary and format are further complicated by rhythm and other poetic device choices. If your Self is close to your everyday Self, your rhythm is likely to be iambic, and if your purpose is serious, your line length will probably be pentameter. Humor, on the other hand, may have a shorter line and a rhythm calculated to move faster, perhaps anapestic. You may allow your subject to flow with a free verse form, or you may hone it into the fine discipline of a Petrarchan sonnet.

Your code will also be influenced by your skill and talent, both of which can improve with practice. For example, Dixie envies her husband's ease with rhyming couplets. "My rhymes keep calling attention to themselves instead of to what the poem says," she fumes. She leans to Anglo-Saxon alliterative four-stress verse, a good complement to her favorite role as the ordinary spiritual psychic next door.

Audience

Audiences for poetry both read and listen. There's something special about hearing poetry read or recited by the author, but most poetry will be published in print rather than orally. Even so, the auditory components of poetry dominate the reader. That's why, in your decisions about Self, defining your voice is so important.

Those protests about writing for themselves and having no audience in mind that we hear from fiction writers are even louder from poets. Unconsciously, audience probably has its appropriate impact, but a poet's audience is usually narrower than a fiction writer's. Poets do indeed write for themselves, or for people like themselves. They can surrender more easily, then, to the Muse within and lose themselves to the poetic principle.

Experience

Sensory detail may be more important in poetry than in any other form of writing. The prosody books will give you good exercises and advice for developing both your observations and your skills in choosing exact words. You may find the sub-modality checklists on the Designer State Worksheet of value as you seek clearer descriptions of your images. And frankly, all other writing could probably benefit from closer attention to good sensory description.

Organizing

Organizing may also be different for the poet. For a narrative, the organizing principles may be the same. For other poetry, the form often dictates the organization. In short poetry, outlines may be unnecessary, since perspective is easy to keep in a few lines. Indeed, the line structure itself may suggest the relationships of the content of the lines. Our suggestion about using the outline as a kind of net to catch inspiration, during the writing of some other section, is especially applicable for the poet. A line, a phrase, or an image can pop into consciousness any time, any place—and good poets are prepared to catch them. Keep pencil and paper handy at all times.

Writing

Poets often have a special state of mind for writing. Some go into a kind of trance, in which the words to express the image or the emotion come more easily. Instead of the compulsive state you used to get yourself all the way through a first draft, you might remember a time when you felt especially inspired, when the lines poured forth in perfect cadence, when the images were so vivid they seemed to leap from your mind to the page. If you've never quite gotten that much of the milk of paradise, imagine what it would be like if you did. Then get into it and anchor that state to use in writing.

Evaluating And Revising

Evaluating and revising have an extra step for poetry. Evaluate and revise first for idea and then for form, just as you would in any other writing. Then evaluate once more for idea. Since poetry is so tightly knit, altering a stitch can alter the fit of the whole garment.

Although all writing is to some extent creative, literary writing offers the broadest scope for your creative powers. And with the POWER writing model, you'll be creating more writing. We'll be looking forward to reading it!

Chapter Ten

POWER In School Writing

Writing can be a very powerful tool for learning. Unfortunately, for many people, school writing seems to be mostly busy work, and that's always a signal of a problem. We'll suggest ways to solve some of these problems and ways to work around them when they're insoluble. This chapter shows you how to make the writing you do in school work for you—efficiently, effectively, and comfortably.

Students write for two reasons, which sometimes overlap and are sometimes quite separate. One reason, and the one most people think of when they think of writing and school, is to demonstrate knowledge and understanding, usually for an evaluation or grade of some sort. A second reason is to learn something, to clarify thinking, or to preserve some ideas to build on later. We'll take you through the POWER model for each kind of writing.

A note on timing is warranted here. If you picked up this book simply for this chapter, thinking that you can learn all you need to know right here, it's time to rethink. Everything we'll be presenting here assumes you're familiar with the POWER model. You'll also find the advice in the chapter on business writing applicable to school papers, since some of what you're doing is selling the teacher on your progress as a student. And if your problem is getting yourself interested in those boring assignments that seem to have no function whatsoever, the section on fiction writing may be helpful.

WRITING FOR EVALUATION

Term papers, essay questions, and themes are typical of the kinds of writing teachers ask students to do for evaluation. Ideally, such writing assignments are given an artificial context that resembles the real-world situation in which such information would be transmitted. In other words, the teacher will ask you to role-play a professional simulation or respond to a "what would you write in a letter to... if you were asked about...." In most schools, however, you may have to create your own context to make the writing most productive. Either way, underlying the assignment is always the context of someone using your writing to evaluate your learning. Here's how the POWER model can help.

Previewing

Self, your role, is already partially defined by the school context. You are a student. Your teacher may have some preconceived ideas about what that means about you as a person. You may want to accept those ideas, or you may want to define the kind of student and person you are differently and more specifically. To make the most of this situation, you need to understand how your teacher sees students.

Most teachers assume they know more than their students. Generally, that's true; they've usually lived longer and had more experience, if nothing else. And since they're in the teacher's role and you're in the student's, their assumption that they know more about the subject of the class is usually valid. That may not always be true, especially when adults return to the classroom. And there will certainly be some topics, perhaps outside of the subject of the class, that you do indeed know more about than the teacher does.

This edge in experience and knowledge gives teachers confidence and competence—and helps them feel safe. Teachers who genuinely want students to surpass them in knowledge and skill, to become the teacher in effect, are rare exceptions. Although that's part of the goal of teaching, when it actually happens, you can see what sort of awkward complications that could make for the teacher's role. It doesn't have to be uncomfortable, though. A competent teacher can easily evaluate the next level above. But teachers don't often get the chance. Having a student willing, even eager, to go beyond the requirements is also a rare exception. When students and teachers approach each other with mutual respect, regardless of the levels of expertise, both roles are more fun, and more learning takes place on both sides.

As you define your student image, we suggest you make respect a major characteristic. Present yourself and your ideas as worthy of respect. Sid learned a terrific rule for dealing with people who are evaluating you, especially people who are expecting to place you in an inferior position: "Treat everyone as if you absolutely expect them to treat you with great respect." When you presuppose you know what you're talking (or writing) about, the only logical response from others is to act respectfully. This attitude is, however, a great responsibility. If you take it on, you must be prepared to deliver on the promise.

In your paper, then, using the information and approaches the teacher expects the very best students to use, you want to deliver a strong sense of your knowledge of the information presented. You may decide to present yourself as a student who knows less than the teacher but who is trying very hard to learn what the teacher has assigned. You may decide to present yourself as a student who is expert, from experience and/or research, on the subject. In any case, your role is ultimately one of a person who is going to get a high grade because you deserve it. Once you commit yourself to that level of self-respect, your tasks are first to learn or gather the information you want to present and then to communicate to your teacher the fact that you do indeed have command of that information.

Knowing the information is one task; communicating that you know is another task entirely. Your primary *purpose* in a school paper is to communicate to the teacher that you know and understand the material you've been learning. Ideally, any test or examination procedure should be a learning experience in itself, in addition to measuring previously acquired knowledge. Good teachers try to design assignments so that knowledge is reinforced, understanding can be measured, and new learning continues. Few things gladden a teacher's heart more than finding proof that their efforts are yielding good results, discovering that a student has learned from as assignment. If you can show your teachers that they have accomplished something by giving the assignment—i.e., gotten you to learn something you didn't already know—you'll most certainly get their attention.

You need also to understand the teacher's specific purpose in giving the assignment, especially if you have some choice about topic and/or approach. What is the pedagogical purpose, the teaching/learning that is supposed to result from the assignment? If you don't know, ask. Ask carefully. Defensive teachers may see this question as an accusation of giving busy work or a whiny, shirker attitude ("Why do we have to do this?"). You might try something like this: "I'd like to make sure I understand the assignment and what we're trying to accomplish. You want us to demonstrate our understanding of the social, political, and economic factors influencing the initial positions of the armies in the Civil War. Is that right? Do we need to include a discussion of field leadership as well?" Or in a less structured situation, something like this: "You want us to show that we understand adapting information to different audiences. Are there also specific format techniques you want to see?"

Your primary *audience* for a school paper is your teacher. The respect you have for yourself must be balanced by respect for your audience. After all, part of respecting yourself is giving your communication efforts to deserving people. You can also assume in most cases that the teacher wants you to do well, wants to discover that you're learning what's being taught. The students' learning is the measure of the teacher's success: if you do well, the teacher has done well. Beyond those preliminaries, though, what do you know about this particular teacher's biases and preferences? As in all good writing, careful audience analysis can be crucial and calls for some serious questions and honest answers.

What is your teacher's attitude toward assignments, this one in particular? Some teachers give assignments because they must, but their hearts are not truly in them. They feel that the real learning comes from class and through reading and thinking, but they must have some relatively objective way of assigning you a grade. Sometimes teachers have been assigned to assign you the project, with little or no voice in what or how the assignment is designed. In fact, the paper may be as much of a chore to the teacher as it seems to you. On the other hand, many teachers are excited about their assignments. They take time to design one they think will accomplish their pedagogical purposes and allow you some creativity and fun in doing the work. They are often disappointed when students don't take the opportunities they've offered to enjoy what they're doing. In any of these cases, how can you make reading your paper a pleasant surprise for the teacher?

What kind of students does your teacher like or appreciate most? What kind of students get the best response in class? Do those students get good grades from the teacher, or are they just getting "pats on the head" to be quiet? How does the teacher respond to you, personally? Is that response a reflection of who the teacher is, or who you are (i.e., how you behave in class)? Can you use this response to your advantage in your paper? If not, can you adjust your paper so that the teacher will respond differently to the image presented in your paper?

In an essay exam, you have few options in the content of your writing, but with themes, term papers, and theses, you may have a great deal of flexibility. What topics might interest the teacher? What things did the teacher concentrate on in class? What "turns the teacher on," and what kinds of things does the teacher consider a waste of time? What could you put in your paper that you're certain your teacher would respond well to (be equally certain that it's appropriate for your paper)? The examples your teacher gives may provide excellent clues for shaping your topic. If the teacher gives several examples, all different, suggesting a variety of topics and approaches, you can assume your creativity and personal interests will be respected. If all the examples have a single theme, a religious overtone, for example, you'd best make your paper follow the example as closely as possible.

As in all other writing, having your audience (your teacher) clearly in mind will help tremendously. Sometimes, though, the thought of being graded gets so tangled up with the image of the reader that people get intimidated just thinking about writing for a teacher. If that image scares you to death, review our earlier discussion on how to handle a hostile audience. One of the best defenses when dealing with people we're apprehensive about is to know how they work on the inside. The chapter on business correspondence has a thorough outline for audience analysis. If you can assess your teacher on the levels of wants and needs, ways of handling problems and challenges, viewing the world, and operating in their relationships with others, you'll have a great advantage in presenting any information. If you can match, in your own mind, the way your teacher thinks, you can answer most of your questions about how to proceed with your paper.

The *code* you use is often built into the assignment. In a technical subject, of course you must use the technical terms. Be sure to use them accurately and spell them correctly. Use the jargon appropriate to the subject and the level of the class you're in. If you're unsure about the degree of technicality or how extensively you can use the jargon, use your teacher's language as your guide. As in any other writing, keep the vocabulary level appropriate for your audience. Don't write down to the teacher, but don't use polysyllabic elaborations unnecessarily, either. Remember that your purpose is to communicate your high status as a student as directly and clearly as possible.

Often, part of the evaluation of a school paper involves format. As you determine that part of your code, pay attention to the structural details and finished appearance. Ask to see some examples if you're in a completely new situation. For example, book report covers with your own art work may be a strong plus for middle school and high school, but college teachers may not appreciate the decoration. Similarly, the apparatus necessary for a master's thesis (table of contents, list of figures, etc.) would be overkill for a three- to five-page research essay.

As you gather your *experience* for the content of your paper, your assignment may have built-in restrictions. You may be limited to material discussed in class or presented in your textbooks, as in essay tests, for example. Or you may be required to research other people's ideas to add to class information and your own interpretations. Often you'll have the option of staying with class information or adding your own personal experience and/or researched information.

Turning an overnight theme assignment into a major research project would be inappropriate, but going beyond merely regurgitating the teacher's information is a clear signal to the teacher that you're a thinking, serious student. Mentioning the relationship of the topic to something you heard on the news, an article or book you read, or a professional in the field you talked to makes your paper more interesting to both you and the teacher. You'll want to be careful to insert your additions appropriately, making sure you aren't implying you know more than the teacher. You're simply sharing the fact that the class information has stimulated your interest and you've found it relevant in other situations. Always credit your sources carefully and clearly, and take care to observe all the conventions that indicate when you're referring to someone else's ideas and whether you are quoting directly or paraphrasing.

If your assignment clearly calls for research beyond your personal experience and class information, give consideration to the validity of your sources, including the kinds of sources your teacher prefers. Scientific fields rely on publications of conference proceedings and on journal articles more than books, for example.

It can take two or three years for a book to be published, by which time the information may well be outdated. Conference proceedings offer the most current information, with journal articles in between.

Interviews can be a great source for research. An expert's opinion or the experience of a professional in the field can give your paper that cutting edge of currency and immediacy. It's also more interesting to you to know your source personally, to have a face to associate with your footnotes. Interviewing does, however, take special preparation and may take more time than traditional library research. Few students, then, take the time and trouble to make use of interviews. If your source clearly provides unique information pertinent to your topic, your paper is likely to be unique as well.

If you're researching a subject you know little about, go first to the more general sources to inform yourself. Then, as soon as possible, focus your topic. Get a good firm thesis statement. That focus will prevent your taking unnecessary notes and getting bogged down into endless research. Take notes on all that might be useful, but be aware that an unfocused thesis means you'll be taking lots of useless notes—wasting your time and notecards.

Creating A Context

One of the drawbacks of many school assignments is that they are just that—school assignments. They are intended to help you learn something, but their connection with your life and the things you care about seems nebulous, at best. Creating an artificial context can make a routine grind come alive and mean something to you.

In some classes it's easy. Maybe you have to write a report on solvents. You imagine you are a chemical supplier, and you're writing a report of solvents you have available, recommending the one most suitable to your prospective client's need. Maybe you have to write a comparison/contrast paper. You check out camcorders, comparing weight, zoom power, warranties, sight flexibility, etc. Then write a letter to your parents explaining why you'd really like to find a particular camcorder model under the Christmas tree. In each of these situations, your Self, Purpose, Audience, Code, and Experience are realistic simulations of things of interest to you and situations you're likely to encounter.

You still have the teacher as your real audience, but you can reserve the teacher for the Evaluating stage, as you might a secondary audience.

Sometimes, though, it isn't so neat and tidy. You may not be able to create a realistic context in which you would actually write about some subjects. Even a partial context can help, though. Let's use one of Dixie's clients to illustrate.

Pete's assignment in the seventh-grade English class was to compare two friends. "Why?" Dixie asked. Pete didn't know. He'd been given no more information than that. And he hadn't been able to get any further than picking the two friends. He had no idea what the assignment was supposed to accomplish, and he didn't know where to start comparing. Dixie pointed out the value of noticing similarities and differences in various situations, explaining its importance in developing evaluative thinking skills. These kinds of things can mean life or death in the jungle. But Dixie didn't have any clues either about the specific outcomes the teacher wanted in this assignment. What kind of details should be compared? And why?

Together they generated some possibilities. Suppose Pete was trying to decide which friend he wanted to invite to spend the day this Saturday. Which one liked the kinds of activities Pete liked, that the two of them could do together, on a Saturday at home, in any kind of weather? In another possibility, suppose Pete had had a growth spurt and could pass his outgrown clothes to his shorter friends. Which one would like which clothes, and why? Who would get the really cool jams, and who would get the button down shirt? Or suppose Pete's cousin in another town wanted a pen pal. Which one would he like better? Or maybe Pete was sending a note to one of the two. How would the messenger know which one should get the note?

Pete ruled out the messenger as too superficial and the penpal as too complicated, since he'd have to compare the friends and the cousin. The Saturday companion would get at their personalities and their abilities, but it wasn't all that interesting. Pete decided to go with the clothes, since that could involve both their personalities and their appearance. The context was still incomplete; there was no logical audience for a written paper on this subject. Certainly the teacher had no real interest in or need to know any of this. But the partial context—a Self (Saturday loafer, second-hand clothier, match-maker, note-sender) and a Purpose— gave Pete a focus for the paper and the kind of "hook," or thesis-interest the teacher wanted.

Pete's next assignment was an essay on "My Most Prized Possessions," and he'd been given the same vague guidelines ("about 300 words"). What about giving someone a tour of his room? Or trying to give someone a subtle hint about what kind of birthday present he'd like? He settled on a more complex situation: what would he save if a hurricane were headed this way? One of his favorite possessions, the television set, was easily replaceable. He settled on saving his money (which could take care of replacing most of the other things he cared about), his baseball card collection, and his photographs.

Before the prized possessions paper was due, however, he got back his comparison-contrast essay. "Not exactly what I had in mind," she told him. Her response was a strong signal for a rethink of the prized possessions. Her one example of a thesis sentence had been, "My most prized possessions are my friends, my family, and my faith." He decided to follow her model as closely as possible. His opening reviewed his favorite possessions, but his "hook" was that his most prized possessions could not be seen. He used her outline for a three-paragraph development—friends, family, and faith—and concluded with a reference to Luke 12:33: "Lay not up for yourself treasures on earth, where moth and dust doth corrupt, but lay up for yourselves treasures in heaven." He'd analyzed his audience; he got his A.

Organizing

Often the teacher will tell you, directly, how the paper should be organized, how long it should be, and how it should look. Such specific instruction certainly makes your job easier, provided the teacher's guidelines are sensible and you use them appropriately. Number of sources usually indicates a minimum. Format is usually dependent on the context—e.g., formal research report for graduate school; handwritten, one side of the page, ink, notebook paper for middle and high schools; typed business letter or memo for progress reports in business-oriented courses.

Length is most people's first consideration, since it's the first indicator of how much work is supposed to go into the project and how much time must be budgeted. However, length is a product of the other decisions you have to make, so the teacher's answer at that point is only a guideline. Dixie used to give this answer to the inevitable question: "Long enough to accomplish your purpose and not a bit longer." In other words, it depends on your previewing and the assignment context. To be fair, Dixie always followed that answer with a ballpark range. And she insisted on prior approval of her students' subjects and purposes, to make sure they weren't tackling more than could be comfortably done in the course limits and that their efforts would indeed accomplish the purposes of the assignment. Sid once had a graduate school instructor set a strict limit on how long a paper should be. When Sid's development of the topic took him over the limit, he wasn't sure how the teacher would react. In the end he was penalized for leaving too much out. If he'd asked Dixie's advice, she'd have told him to consult the teacher, saying something like this: "My paper purpose is...I've developed these main ideas...to this extent...I'd like to include...but that would take me over the page number limit. What do you suggest?"

The suggestions in the chapter on Organizing should help you handle the rest of the decisions you'll need to make here. Remember that you can always borrow someone else's strategy for organizing a school paper. That's why teachers give you models. In fact, you are often expected to copy someone else's structure and format. There's a clear distinction here between a general structure and someone's ideas or words. Carefully credit ideas and words to your source. And if the structure you borrow is unusual, credit your source with that, too.

Writing, Evaluating, And Revising

The Writing, Evaluating, and Revising steps of the POWER model are much the same for school papers as for any other kind of writing. In some ways, they may be easier. Since you are usually writing for an audience of one (your teacher), for instance, that's the person you have in mind as you evaluate.

As you might do in organizing, you can borrow a writing style from someone else, too. Who else has presented similar information in a way that you (and your teacher) like? Learn from that example. A writing style develops over a period of time, and changes according to the context of the writing. One of the best ways of developing your own style is to begin by imitating writers you admire.

Give Proofseeing special attention in school papers. That first impression can make a big difference in how your ideas are received. You can assume that grammar and mechanics will be given great importance, even in classes outside of English. School papers are, after all, supposed to demonstrate your ability, knowledge, and care in presenting your work. Some teachers are more sticky about these things than others, but no one has ever been penalized for getting it all right. If you work with a computer, use all the tools available—spell checker, readability measures, etc. Don't, however, expect the computer to simply do it for you; if you use the wrong word but spell it right, the computer won't catch the resulting misinformation.

Choosing A Topic

If you have freedom of choice, your topic can be your biggest asset in a school paper—or your worst liability. Here are a few guidelines on choosing well.

A subject you are interested in is of utmost importance. You're going to have to spend some time with it; make it worth your while and as pleasant as possible. You may, however, want to avoid anything you're blindly passionate about if there's any room for disagreement, since it might be difficult for you to present the other side objectively.

Controversial subjects can be a source of lively debate. They are, however, very hard to handle well. Generally, we suggest you avoid them. If your teacher turns out to be on the other side of the controversy, you may be in trouble before you begin. If your teacher is passionately partisan and you know the bias, you may still be penalized for omitting important supporting details known only to the experts. Or the teacher may think you are simply writing what you assume to be the teacher's opinions, and that can be insulting. Furthermore, many controversial subjects that are new to students and certainly worth thought and debate (capital punishment and abortion, for example) are old and worn to the teacher. Unless you've found a genuinely fresh approach, your paper will simply blend into the years-long stream.

When you do deal with a controversial topic, make sure you present all the relevant aspects of the argument, as fairly and accurately as possible (unless, of course, your role and purpose—with the teacher's full support—call for you to present a biased case.) Looking at television news or reading a good newspaper can show you how this is done. Notice the difference between the way an anchor person, for example, reads the news and the way a commentator states "the opinion of the station." And notice that it becomes easy to tell when the reporters' biases are showing. Notice the same differences in the newspaper between the feature news stories and the editorial page. Your biases will probably show just as clearly.

One approach is to state your own opinion up front and then explain how you carefully reasoned your way to that conclusion. If you're still in a dilemma about your presentation, discuss the problem with your teacher. Such a conference can prepare you and also your teacher for the final paper.

When you have only choices you don't really like or when you feel stuck in a no-win situation, you might try changing the rules of the game somehow. This isn't always easy, but it can make all the difference if you can take the time to be creative and artful. Sid used this tactic in graduate school several times. His classes were quite large, and the teachers often assigned the same basic paper to everyone in the class. Sid usually found these canned assignments very dull and sometimes insultingly simple. So he would approach his teachers with an offer to do a "more advanced" paper than the rest of the class. He would pick some topic clearly germane to the course but indeed more sophisticated than the teachers expected the rest of the class to be able to handle. His personalization of the assignments accomplished several things. First, it gave his teachers the strong impression that they were dealing with an unusual student. Second, the teachers got a chance to help him shape the assignments into something they might be particularly interested in. Third, the teachers got a break from the monotony of reading thirty or more of the same paper over and over. Fourth, the teachers couldn't compare Sid's papers directly with all the others in the class. Finally, and most important to Sid, it gave him something far more interesting to explore.

Creating your own context falls into this category of rule changing. Use this technique judiciously, but considering the options can help you do a better job with the original task if you decide that's best. This kind of assessment of yourself, your teacher and the assignment, will make your job more straightforward and logical. It can also teach you to think in larger terms than just doing a paper to get through a class. Education is much more than that. Use your savvy to get the kind of learning you want, along with that good grade, and sell yourself as a person who is writing from firm knowledge, beyond the shadow of a doubt.

WRITING TO LEARN

Ideally, school is primarily for learning. You've probably been using writing as a learning tool when you take notes or outline potential exam questions before a test, but you may not be using it as effectively as you can when you become aware of its power and begin to take full advantage of the POWERful process. When you write purely to improve your own knowledge or thinking skills, the process of writing can differ markedly from the process you'll use in writing that will be evaluated. Mostly it's shorter.

Previewing

Major differences in Previewing mark writing purely for learning with no evaluation attached. Your *Self* and your *Audience* are the same, probably the only time you really and truly write just for yourself. How you define your Self depends in part on what you want to learn. You're a student, yes, but a student of what? And how willingly? If you're interested in your subject and want to learn it, your Self is fairly well defined.

If the answer to that last question is about zero to three on a willingness scale of one to ten, you might find the fiction writing section useful. Do consider creating a context for it that touches your life somehow. It's not easy to learn something you don't want to learn, see no use for, and don't like. It's possible, but it's not fun. Think about who might genuinely want to learn this? What could it be used for? If you really have no ideas for answering these two questions, ask your teacher (politely, of course). Then imagine what it would be like to be in the position of a person needing and wanting to learn this. Stretch a little further and find some similarities between that person and your own life. If you still can't make any personal connection between your real life and your subject, try role playing.

Your *Purpose* for writing is, of course, primarily to learn, and while you're in school, much of your learning is simply because someone tells you to. Some things are indeed worth learning just for their own sakes. However, learning is more fun and efficient when it's purposeful. You need a purpose for learning beyond "because it's going to be on the test." If you have a strong interest in your subject, you probably already have a good purpose for learning. How does this topic, this subject, this class fit with the other things you're learning in school? What's its relation to the things you do and care about outside of school? What connection does it have to what you want to be doing later in life? If you can connect it to a larger purpose that matters to you, you're halfway there.

Your *Code* may be radically different when you write for yourself for personal learning. Outlines, especially the more visual forms of outlines like mapping and flow charts, may be the format you need. When you're taking notes, either from lecture or reading, leave extra space to add notes later for more depth. Make use of subject headings and color coding to coordinate notes from several sources. The caution in the chapter on *Writing* about using one side of the page only, may be especially useful here. As you spread out all your notes, with headings color-coded into the margins, you want to be able to see everything there is.

Organizing

For study, the major organizing task is to get all your ideas and notes on one topic together, then to see the relationships between and among them. It may stop there. If you're going to have a short answer or multiple-guess quiz, that may be all you need. But if you'll have essay exams or if your teacher is very skilled at multiple-guess test-making, you need to consider the relationships between the topics. Lean heavily on the visual approaches to organizing suggested in that chapter. The more clearly you can see connections between pieces of information, the easier it will be to remember it.

Writing

You might not need to write at all when you are writing to learn. You're writing, of course, but a draft of some document may be completely irrelevant.

Evaluating And Revising

Your evaluation viewpoint may be different in writing to learn. You have the same two vantage points you need to consider. Your first criterion is whether or not you know what you need to know. Your second is whether or not you know what the teacher thinks you ought to know, if you're in a school situation. Learning on your own gives you great freedom in choosing your scope and purpose. But learning with a teacher can give you guidance in how much, and of what, you need to learn to accomplish your purpose. As you assess that part of your preparation thus far, think about what kinds of information and linkage of information will be necessary for this teacher's tests.

Learning/Writing

Ultimately, all writing leads to some kind of learning. Once you realize both the inevitability of the outcome in the tool and the versatility of the tool in the outcome, you're back in control: when you write, you're going to learn something; when you want to learn something, writing can help. Using the POWER Process can make it all more efficient, more effective and more fun.

Part IV
Appendices

Appendices

Appendix I

Designer State Worksheets

Here are two versions of the Designer State Worksheet, both exactly the same except for space. Use the two-page version if your handwriting is large or you like plenty of room for your notes. The one-page version used in the text, follows. There are two copies of each version included here. Feel free to make as many copies as you need.

You may also, as you play with designing states to suit your needs, want to develop your own worksheet, giving more space to those modalities and sub-modalities that have the most impact for you. It's a good idea to consider, at least briefly, all the possibilities, however. You never know when a little-noticed sub-modality might have surprisingly powerful influence.

DESIGNER STATE WORKSHEET

Descriptive Label For State Of Consciousness:

Description Of Content:

Visual Form:

Brightness	Movement/Speed
Size	Location
Color/Black & White	Associated/Disassociated
Distance	Frame/No Frame
3 Dimensional/Flat	Focus
Shape	Clarity
Contrast	Slide/Photo/Motion Picture
Direction	Other?

Auditory Form:

Sounds	Distance
Words	Timbre
Music	Tones
Voices (Whose?)	Pitch
Volume	Location
Duration	Internal/External
Rhythm	Tempo
Other?	

Kinesthetic Form:

Emotion	Temperature
Internal	External
Weight	Duration
Size	Pressure
Frequency	Tactile
Proprioceptive	Shape
Movement	Intensity
Moisture	Texture
Rhythm	Balance
Muscle tension	Breathing
Location	
Other?	

Olfactory/Gustatory Form:

Sweet	Pungent
Sour	Intensity
Salty	Location
Bitter	Aromatic
Specific Taste	Specific Smell

Anchor:

DESIGNER STATE WORKSHEET

Descriptive Label For State Of Consciousness:

Description Of Content:

Visual Form:

Brightness	Movement/Speed
Size	Location
Color/Black & White	Associated/Disassociated
Distance	Frame/No Frame
3 Dimensional/Flat	Focus
Shape	Clarity
Contrast	Slide/Photo/Motion Picture
Direction	Other?

Auditory Form:

Sounds	Distance
Words	Timbre
Music	Tones
Voices (Whose?)	Pitch
Volume	Location
Duration	Internal/External
Rhythm	Tempo
Other?	

Kinesthetic Form:

Emotion	Temperature
Internal	External
Weight	Duration
Size	Pressure
Frequency	Tactile
Proprioceptive	Shape
Movement	Intensity
Moisture	Texture
Rhythm	Balance
Muscle tension	Breathing
Location	
Other?	

Olfactory/Gustatory Form:

Sweet	Pungent
Sour	Intensity
Salty	Location
Bitter	Aromatic
Specific Taste	Specific Smell

Anchor:

DESIGNER STATE WORKSHEET

Descriptive Label For State Of Consciousness:

Description Of Content:

Visual Form:

Brightness	Movement/Speed
Size	Location
Color/Black & White	Associated/Disassociated
Distance	Frame/No Frame
3 Dimensional/Flat	Focus
Shape	Clarity
Contrast	Slide/Photo/Motion Picture
Direction	Other?

Auditory Form:

Sounds	Distance
Words	Timbre
Music	Tones
Voices (Whose?)	Pitch
Volume	Location
Duration	Internal/External
Rhythm	Tempo
Other?	

Kinesthetic Form:

Emotion	Temperature
Internal	External
Weight	Duration
Size	Pressure
Frequency	Tactile
Proprioceptive	Shape
Movement	Intensity
Moisture	Texture
Rhythm	Balance
Muscle tension	Breathing
Location	
Other?	

Olfactory/Gustatory Form:

Sweet	Pungent
Sour	Intensity
Salty	Location
Bitter	Aromatic
Specific Taste	Specific Smell

Anchor:

DESIGNER STATE WORKSHEET

Descriptive Label For State Of Consciousness:

Description Of Content:

Visual Form:

Brightness

Size

Color/Black & White

Distance

3 Dimensional/Flat

Shape

Contrast

Direction

Movement/Speed

Location

Associated/Disassociated

Frame/No Frame

Focus

Clarity

Slide/Photo/Motion Picture

Other?

Auditory Form:

Sounds

Words

Music

Voices (Whose?)

Volume

Duration

Rhythm

Other?

Distance

Timbre

Tones

Pitch

Location

Internal/External

Tempo

Kinesthetic Form:

Emotion

Internal

Weight

Size

Frequency

Proprioceptive

Movement

Moisture

Rhythm

Muscle tension

Location

Other?

Temperature

External

Duration

Pressure

Tactile

Shape

Intensity

Texture

Balance

Breathing

Olfactory/Gustatory Form:

Sweet

Sour

Salty

Bitter

Specific Taste

Pungent

Intensity

Location

Aromatic

Specific Smell

Anchor:

Appendix II

Unblocking Your POWER: Answers To Your Problems

Although people who follow the POWER Process for writing seldom have writer's block, it does happen occasionally. In this chapter, we'll suggest ways of dealing with your writer's block, first generally and then at specific stages in the writing process.

IDENTIFY THE CAUSE

Eliminating a problem is always easier if you can identify the cause. Sometimes the cause is directly related to the stage in the process. For example, you get stuck in writing the first draft because you've let your evaluating critic go to work too early. We'll attack those more specifically later. Two generalized causes, however, can produce writer's block at any stage.

The first culprit is confusing the product and the process. Writing is a process. Any time you start expecting perfect product in the first three stages, you're going to get yourself stuck or, at the very least, make writing a much more difficult and unpleasant task than need be. Simply remind yourself that you are in the middle of a process and take note of what state would really be appropriate for your in-process product. The second culprit is anxiety. Likely sources of anxiety during specific stages of the process have been mentioned in Part I, but it can pop up anywhere.

ELIMINATE THE BLOCK

Although specific blocks can be eliminated more easily than general ones, we suggest three main strategies to cope with generalized writer's block—or blocks to anything else you're trying to accomplish.

Check Your Body

The block may be physical, in the form of unnecessary muscular tension. Check your breathing first. When you forget to breathe, all sorts of things happen—all of them unpleasant. Your brain needs oxygen to function, and to get oxygen to the brain, you have to breathe!

Now relax the rest of your body. Move with your breathing to release tight joints and muscles. Check your body from top to toe for excess tension. Shake it out, or let it flow away gently. Take another deep slow breath, let it out slowly, and return to work refreshed.

Change Your State

Changing your body posture and your breathing will inevitably change your state. Of course, you now have the tools to make that kind of change more specifically and directly. Simply use one of your previously prepared Designer State Worksheets as an anchor to get back to a productive state. Or get a fresh worksheet and design a new, more flexible and creative state.

Objectify The Block

Writer's block is so nebulous. We notice the results—no writing being done. But the block itself is simply a set of feelings and attitudes, which sometimes seem to creep back despite deep breathing and detailed worksheets. The block is easier to deal with if we can objectify it, put it outside ourselves, either physically or mentally. Or both.

When Dixie's husband was writing his first master's thesis, he got a bad case of writer's block. Finally, Dixie presented him with his own personal objective writer's block: a walnut wood block. With it went these instructions: "When you're ready to write and can't, place your writer's block on the edge of your desk—and KNOCK IT OFF!"

To objectify a block mentally, you might use the following worksheet:

UNBLOCKING WRITER'S BLOCK

How do you know when you have writer's block?

If you could objectify your writer's block, how would you describe it?

How would it look?

How would it feel?

Does it make any sound?

Think of a time when your writer's block was gone, when you wrote comfortably, easily, and freely, when you actually enjoyed writing. How would you describe that time?

Here's the way Katherine filled hers out:

How do you know when you have writer's block?

> fidgety
> frustrated

If you could objectify your writer's block, how would you describe it?

> undirected energy   destructive
> ungrounded charge

How would it look?

How would it feel?

> cloudy

Does it make any sound?

> static

Think of a time when your writer's block was gone, when you wrote comfortably, easily, and freely, when you actually enjoyed writing. How would you describe that time?

> secure   excited
> talking in my head   hearing words

Katherine's block was easily changed, despite the fierceness of her images. She simply imagined the lightening bolt firing its energy down into her creative mind and pictured the cloud turning pink and breaking up into little feathery mists.

UNBLOCK THROUGHOUT THE PROCESS

We usually begin a seminar or workshop by surveying participants' problems to make sure we'll get them all taken care of
before it's over. This section coordinates the results of those
surveys with the writing process and suggests specific solutions
to the problems.

Problems Getting Started

I can't get started. A blank page makes me go blank.
Begin Previewing by answering the SPACE questions, or use a
plan sheet.

*My writing seems confused at first, like I don't know what I'm saying.
What I write at the beginning is unrelated to what I really want to say,
although it gets better as I go along.*
Writing randomly is a good warm-up exercise for some
people. If you'd rather warm up more efficiently, however,
check your SPACE, especially the SPA components.

*I'm uncomfortable doing the project. It brings up old memories I'd
rather forget. But it's got to be done.*
*I'm immediately reminded, unpleasantly, of school writing assignments
and tests.*
My emotions are in the way, I get upset, angry, etc.
A clearer SPACE, especially the SPA, may be all that's needed
here. But you may need to create a better mental atmosphere
for yourself to begin with. Use anchoring to recreate a more
pleasant, productive state of mind, and then Preview your
SPACE.

My thoughts are too scattered.
I'm overwhelmed by the size of the project, the limited time, etc.
I lack focus.
While these complaints can often be eased by the advice just
above, they may also respond to sub-modality adjustments.
Pictures that are moving too fast, loom too large, or pull in too
close can be very uncomfortable. Lack of focus may be literally
that.

I don't know enough.

Genuine lack of knowledge will show up as you collect your Experience in Previewing, or as you Organize your information. With a clear SPACE, you should have an indication of the specific knowledge you need to gain to proceed. If the information is there, however, but the feeling of ignorance remains, you may simply be suffering from a lack of confidence. Go back to your Self, and anchor in a little more confidence.

Other things have priority.
Urgent things get in the way of the important things.
I just keep procrastinating.

Well, what is the value of this writing task? Just how important is it, and what time frame do you have for it? Are there, perhaps, emotional blocks masquerading here, or is it simply a matter of setting personal priorities? Remember that the POWER Process can streamline other tasks, too. And a good bit of Previewing and Organizing can be done while you're doing other chores.

Problems With Audience Or Other People's Expectations

There's a difference between what I want to say and what's expected of me.
I don't know what my reader wants.
It's hard to satisfy somebody else's criteria.

Go back to Previewing and look at the audience needs. If you don't have enough information to clarify those needs, you need to get it. It's not impossible to satisfy somebody else's needs and standards if you don't know what they are, but your chances are as good as a shot in the dark. And that's generally a waste of time.

Put yourself in your audience's reading glasses, so to speak. What will you need to satisfy your reason for reading? Many people make the ogre's criteria harder than necessary. If audience criticism keeps looming, simply move that critical voice to the Evaluating stage of the writing process, where that feedback will be appreciated. If the difference between what you want to say and what's expected stems from a clash between the facts you must report and the reader's hopes, simply take your reader's feelings tactfully into account. But if you're being expected to produce a report on something about which you have no knowledge or no expertise, you need either to pass the writing task on to someone more appropriate or to take the Experience stage of Previewing out into the field and gather your information.

I know what I mean, but will my audience?
I need some feedback, and it's not coming.
I've got different levels to communicate to, more than one audience.
Having a clear Audience will help throughout. Remember to take your understanding of the audience into the Evaluating process. You'll be surprised at how easily you can see and hear from someone else's point of view. After you've evaluated and revised on your own, you may want to get a live member of your audience to evaluate for you. In technical documents, this kind of field testing is essential. And as you juggle multiple audience needs, keep in mind the possibility of multiple documents, or a single basic component with differing cover letters.

Somebody else may have already done this. I may be wasting my time repeating what's been done before.
As you assess your Experience, consider a trip or a call to your library. Ask the reference librarian to show you how to find out what's already been done. Then check your Audience again. If it's been done, but your prospective reader still doesn't know about it, then maybe it needs to be done again from a different perspective. Too, many things bear repeating in new ways. Certainly, it's all right to use other people's experience in your own. Just be careful to give credit appropriately. For a review of how to credit sources and avoid plagiarism, see one of the handbooks recommended in the bibliography.

Once it's on paper, it's permanent.
If I write it, I'm committed to it and can't take it back.
No, it's not, and yes, you can. It's not permanent until you decide you want it to be. You don't have to give what you've written to anybody else if you don't want to. And if you do and later change your mind, you simply produce another version. Or write an update memo. If the problem stems from insecurity about what you have to say, return to Previewing and focus your Purpose. If the problem is insecurity about

how what you say will be received, look again at Audience. And if the sight of words on paper still bothers you, do your composing with a computer, where the words will just scroll away until you're sure you want to keep them.

Problems With Internal Processing Or Discomfort

I can't write fast enough. My thoughts move too fast for my fingers.

Isn't creativity wonderful! How about your tongue? Many people talk their blue streaks into a tape recorder and let the fingers catch up later. But remember, the fingers don't have to get every word and nuance exactly right the first time. You do, however, want to catch and hold every good idea. While you're writing the first draft, remember you can skip parts and come back later to fill in the details or make complete sentences. Use your outline or a side-line outline (paper beside your outline on which you can add notes to yourself about the content) to catch any brilliant ideas you want to save for later. If your thoughts are taking you astray from your main task, you might even want to take time out for just brainstorming—letting all those great ideas pour out while you make notes (Try the mapping techniques for recording the results). You can either incorporate them into your current project if they're appropriate (return to Organizing), or save them for another time. If you don't want to be side-tracked, no matter how good the idea might be, use your outline to keep yourself on target.

The format seems fuzzy.

Your Organizing step may suggest a natural format. Or you may need to return to Previewing and the Code stage. Check with your Audience to see what formats would be applicable.

I have to finish what I start, now,
I have to finish this perfectly, now.

Don't start anything you can't finish? Why not? Some things aren't worth finishing. Dixie recalls a friend's first attempt at a hamburger pie, for instance. And sometimes your purpose can be accomplished before the project is over. Check your Previewing Purpose. Sometimes a project has to go on hold: other projects take temporary priority, new information turns up and must be digested, etc. Writing is a process, and processes take time.

Anything worth doing is worth doing right, right? That's probably true, but don't let not being perfect keep you from the perhaps shaky beginning you need to learn how to do something well. Anything worth doing is also worth doing badly, as you learn how to improve. And remember that writing is a process (some things bear repeating). It's not supposed to spring forth from your head like a perfect goddess. But stay with the process, and it'll take you right toward that perfection you want.

I'm unsure of my skills. I don't have any confidence in my competence.

If your concerns refer to competence in your field and skill in your subject area, return to Previewing. Take a good look at your Self and your qualifications. If your SPACE is intact and you still think the project is worth doing, try anchoring a more confident state of mind to use here.

If your concerns refer to competence in writing, ask your reader. Or get an outside editorial opinion at the Evaluating stage of the process. To find an editor, call an office service, a publishing service, the English or Rhetoric Department of a nearby college, or the Association of Professional Communication Consultants (see bibliography). If you are only mildly shaky, try one of the books suggested in the bibliography. If you need substantial help, take a course or hire a tutor. If you're really desperate, hire someone to do the writing for you. Competence in anything comes with practice. We think writing is a skill with which everyone can—and should—be not only competent but also comfortable. But you don't have to be competent at everything.

Writing gives me a headache.
That kind of concentration is a pain in the neck—and other places.

Make a body check first. Are you breathing? Are your shoulders scrunched up around your ears? Relax and let unnecessary tension slide off. Physical distress often stems from a physical cause. Next make a mental check. Are your pictures too fast, too close, too big? Are you hearing too many voices or sounds, too loud, too fast, too screechy? Internal sub-modalities can create physical discomfort, too.

All those rules about writing have me tied in knots.

Put the rules in their proper place—in the Evaluation step of the writing process. Yep, being concerned about following all the rules while you're Writing that first draft is a good way to tie yourself up.

Problems About Finishing

It's never good enough. I always need to polish it more.

It isn't easy to be objective about your own writing, even with the techniques we suggest. There probably will always be something more that could be improved. So do you want to keep tinkering with it forever, or do you want to stop at an appropriate time and get on with something else? Go back to your Previewing. What criteria must you meet to satisfy your Purpose and your audience needs? When you meet those criteria, you may stop. Or you may have a deadline. In that case, you do the best you can in the time allotted (practice good time management and follow the POWER Process), and hand it over. In real-world writing, things don't often have to be perfect; they just have to be done.

When I finish, it doesn't seem worth anything.

Again, it's hard to be objective about your own writing. Sometimes you look at it and think, "Wow, that's great—just what my reader needs!" Then you look at it again and think, "But that's so obvious and tiresome." Reality is somewhere in between. Keep your SPACE firmly in mind as you Evaluate and Revise. Then it's time to let your document face the world on its own.

I keep thinking of more things I could add.

Dixie once had a client who'd spent four years gathering data and now could no longer put off writing a report of what he'd been doing. He'd used the quest for more knowledge, greater authority, as an excuse to procrastinate on writing. Actually, what he'd researched in the first year could have satisfied the requirements and expectations of his assignment. Now, four years of data accumulation was indeed a formidable task. Go back to your Previewing, Audience and Purpose. When you've satisfied the requirements there, you need to stop. You could recommend further study, if you like. Or you can alter your Purpose. But you need to make that kind of decision deliberately.

I don't know where, how, or if I should publish.

"If", is up to you. "How" and "where" comes from studying the markets and talking to those who know or can actually make those kinds of decisions. The bibliography recommends some starting points.

WRITE FREELY

Even the most experienced and skillful writers are plagued with writer's block from time to time, but we don't have to let the blocks stop us anymore. Just treat your momentary block the way you would any other minor inconvenience, unblock, and get on with the process of writing.

Appendix III

Power POWER User's Guide

This appendix chapter has two purposes. First, it is a set of reminders for the person who has gone through the POWER Process enough to know how to use it but who still feels the need for a "map" of the territory. It is not, however, a substitute for reading the book. Without having read the explanation of each step, you may not be able to follow this guide. After you've read the book, this quick review can further speed your POWER Process.

Second, this chapter is a trouble-shooting guide. The POWER Process itself will eliminate most of the problems you might have with writing. A number of decisions, though, and sometimes some trade-offs, have to be made in any project. This guide will get you through considering all the important parts of designing and carrying through on your project.

Each section begins with a summary of that part of the POWER Process, very like the exercises we took you through in each chapter. Following these instructions, you can complete that step without having to flip through the book to find each exercise.

Then there is a long series of questions to ask yourself about that step. If you're following the POWER Process and still have a problem, it's nearly always because you've left a crucial question unanswered. This section suggests the questions you may need to do a thorough job at each step.

PREVIEWING

Previewing has five interrelated components to help you find the best writing SPACE: *Self, Purpose, Audience, Code,* and *Experience.*

Self

The Process Of Previewing Self
Step 1. Go to Third Position and objectively view yourSelf as you want to be in this context.

Step 2. Make content adjustments.
Make sub-modality adjustments.

Step 3. Go back to First Position and imagine yourself as that Self.
Check your FEELINGS.
If you're comfortable, use the Designer State Worksheet.
If you're uncomfortable, repeat Steps 1-3 as needed.

Step 4. Anchor this Self state. Save your Designer Self State Worksheet.

Questions About Your Self:
- What role am I playing in this project?
- Do I have more than one role? Are they compatible?
- Are any of my roles competing with one another?
- Are any of my roles competing with someone else?
- Is one (or more) of these people my reader?
- Am I choosing a role that will, by its very nature, make my work more difficult ?

- Is there a particular tone, or attitude that goes with this role I've chosen?
- Do I really want this tone or attitude?

- What is my vantage point in this role?
- Why have I chosen it? What is its advantage to me?
- Is it appropriate?

- Have I chosen a role that is comfortable for me? Or is it at least not so uncomfortable or foreign that it will make my work too difficult?
- Does taking on this role produce a worthwhile state for me to be in while I work on this writing project?

- Do I need to fill out a Designer State Worksheet to help me define mySelf?
- Do I need to anchor this role/state?

Purpose

The Process Of Previewing Purpose
Step 1. List all possible Purposes.

Step 2. Question each Purpose, individually.

Step 3. Cross-check each Purpose for compatibility with others.

Step 4. Go to Third Position and see the outcome of your Purpose being accomplished in your reader.

Step 5. Go back to First Position, and check your FEELINGS about seeing your Purpose accomplished.
> If you're comfortable, use a Designer State Worksheet to help you make the content and sub-modality adjustments you need.
> If you're uncomfortable, repeat Steps 1-4 as needed.

Step 6. Anchor the state.

Step 7. Repeat Steps 1-6 for each Purpose, individually, if needed.

Questions About Your Purpose
- Why am I writing this? What is my primary Purpose?
- Do I need to subdivide the Purpose? How? What sequence should subdivision follow?

- How many Purposes do I have? Have I listed them by priority?
- Are they compatible with one another?

- Are they personal, business, professional, or something else?
- Am I trying to impress somebody? Is this the best way to do it?
- Am I trying to develop or enhance a particular relationship with my reader, or with someone else, in writing this?
- Am I trying to solve a problem by writing this?
- Do I want to create a certain attitude, feeling, or other Experience in my reader(s)?
- What specific action do I want my reader to take as a result of reading what I have written?

- Can my Purpose(s) be accomplished in this document?
- Can written communication accomplish my Purpose?
- Would some other means of communication be more appropriate?

- What would it look, sound and feel like when I actually accomplish my Purposes?
- What other results or consequences may stem from accomplishing my Purpose?
- After answering these two questions, do I still think my Purpose is worthwhile?

- Have I chosen a Purpose that is comfortable for me? Or is it at least not so uncomfortable or foreign that it will make my work too difficult?
- Does thinking about this Purpose produce a worthwhile state for me to be in while I work on this writing project?

- Do I need to fill out a Designer State Worksheet to help me define my Purpose?
- Do I need to anchor this state, imagining my Purpose is accomplished?

Audience

The Process Of Previewing Audience

Step 1. Identify your reader by name (or **very** specific character-istics), or list all possible Audience members.

Step 2. Go to Third Position and see yourself presenting your ideas to your reader, or to the **first** Audience member on your list.

Step 3. Go back to First Position and check your FEELINGS while you directly address your Audience.
> If you're comfortable, go on to Step 4.
> If you're uncomfortable, repeat Steps 1 and 2, using a Designer State Worksheet to help you adjust content and sub-modalities.
> If you're still uncomfortable, choose a similar but more comfortable Audience to help you through the first three steps of the writing process. You'll bring back the genuine Audience for Evaluating and Revising.

Step 4. Check the sequence of your reader's response to your presentation, from the beginning all the way through accomplishing your Purpose.
> If it doesn't work, logically or for any other reason, adjust your Self (role), Purpose, or your Audience as needed.

Step 5. Complete the image of your reader.
> If you have only one Audience member, you're finished with this exercise and can go on to consid-ering your Code.
> If you have more than one Audience member, repeat Steps 1-5 for each one remaining.

Step 6. Gather all your Audience members together, and repeat Step 2 by seeing yourself presenting ideas to the entire Audience at once.

Step 7. Repeat Steps 3-5 with the entire Audience, by checking your feelings, making adjustments, and checking to make sure the presentation works logically and every other way for your Audience.

Questions About Your Audience

- Who is my primary Audience for this project?
- Do I have a clear mental image of him/her/them? Can I hear their voices clearly?
- How do I feel about them? Does it matter?
- Do I really know this Audience well enough to write to them? Do I need consultation about them?

- How does my perception of my Audience influence the way I write? Will my attitude and tone be all right?
- Do I need to change my attitude or tone? How?
- If my feelings about my Audience get in my way while I write, can I set those aside while I finish the first three phases of the process, then use them in the revision phase?

- In what context will my Audience read this? What constraints will that put on their reading?
- What is my Audience's Purpose for reading? Is there any conflict between their Purpose and mine? Can any such incompatibility be resolved somehow?

- Is there a secondary Audience? Is it compatible with the primary reader?
- Do I have extremely conflicting Audience members? Can I resolve any conflict? Is it worthwhile to do so?
- Would I be better off choosing another Audience (if possible) or another means of communication?
- Should I write separate pieces to these incompatible Audience members?

- Have I chosen an Audience (do I have a choice?) that I am comfortable with? Do any feelings, attitudes, or ideas I have about them make me feel uneasy or hesitant to write? Will this make my work too difficult?

- Should I imagine an alternative Audience while I write, just to get through the Writing phase, and then return to this one for Evaluating and Revising?
- Does thinking about my Audience produce a worthwhile state for me to be in while I write?
- Do I need to fill out a Designer State Worksheet to help define my Audience?
- Do I need to anchor this state, clearly imagining my Audience?

Code

The Process Of Previewing Code

Step 1. Go to Third Position and watch your reader reading your material. Ask yourself if it seems appropriately formatted and designed.

Step 2. Go back to First Position and directly ask your reader's (listener's) opinion of what you've written (said).

Step 3. Listen to the language your reader uses.

Step 4. Imagine continuing this kind of conversation with your reader and match your language to your reader's.

Step 5. Check your FEELINGS, and make any necessary adjustments, first in content, then in sub-modalities.

Step 6. Repeat Steps 3-5 as needed.

Step 7. If you have only one reader, go on to Experience.
If you have multiple readers, repeat Steps 1-5 for each Audience member.

Step 8. Address the entire Audience again, as a group. Check your FEELINGS and make any necessary adjustments.

Questions About Your Code

- What level of vocabulary is appropriate?
  Fifth grade? High school or college graduate?
  Professional?
  Technical language, lay language, jargon?

- What kind of language would my Audience use? What would they most appreciate?

- What level of formality should I use?
- What format should I use?
- What format would be most convenient for the context in which it will be used?
- Has someone else done what I'm doing? Could I "borrow" an effective format or design from somebody who has already done this?
- How can my choice of format and language enhance my reader's understanding and appreciation of my presentation?
- Would any of these devices clarify my presentation?
  Charts, pictures, graphs, or other visual aids?
  Sidebars, boxes, appendices, or other devices to include pertinent information that may not fit into the main text?
  References or other guides to the reader for further exploration of the ideas?
  An executive summary, table of contents, index, outline, or other guide to help a reader through lengthy or difficult material?
  Headings and subheadings, changes in type style or size, or color changes to more clearly reveal organization?
- Do I need consultation or expert help (graphic artist, for example) in designing this document?

- Have I chosen a Code (do I have some choice?) that I am comfortable with?
  Do I know this "language"?
  Will using it make my work too difficult?
- Does operating in this Code or format produce a worthwhile state for me to be in while I write?
  Would it help me to write this in a more comfortable or familiar Code, just to get through the first three stages of the process, and then later do a "translation"?

- Do I need to fill out a Designer State Worksheet to help me clarify my Code?
- Do I need to anchor the state of imagining communicating directly with my Audience in this Code?

Experience

The Process Of Previewing Experience

Step 1. List all major points or ideas—Experience—for this presentation.

Step 2. Decide the relevance of each. Try them out on your Audience, as you did with Code.

Step 3. Check Audience responses, and your feelings.

Step 4. Make any necessary adjustments. Discard Experiences/ information that is not relevant. Add other pertinent Experience. Note areas where you may need to gather more Experience/information.

Step 5. Repeat steps 2-4 with each major revision in Experience or with each member of your Audience, as needed.

Step 6. Check your list against your Purpose(s). Make sure everything on your list supports your Purpose, and that you have a note about everything you need.

Step 7. Gather any remaining Experience or information you need.

Questions About Your Experience

- Have I listed everything I am aware of that could possibly be relevant to this presentation?

- Do I have enough information to write this?
- If not, where can I get what I need?
  Remembering more personal Experience?
  Library, computer, laboratory, or other research?
  Government, association, industry, or other institutional information sources?
  Personal contacts or interviews with experts or other authors on the subject?
  Television, radio, or other media sources?

- Are my sources of information reliable? Credible?

- Have I tested, in my imagination, each piece of information for relevance to my Purpose?
  Have I discarded any irrelevant or inappropriate pieces?
- Have I tested, in my imagination, each piece of information for relevance and appropriateness to my Audience?
- Have I discarded any ineffective pieces?

- Do I really understand my information?
- Do I have a sense of "ownership" of this Experience?
- Does sharing this Experience or information make me uncomfortable in any way?
- Does it produce a worthwhile state for me to be in while I write?

- Do I need to fill out a Designer State Worksheet to help me define my relevant Experience?
- Do I need to anchor any particular state to help me with my Experience?

ORGANIZING

Since Audience, Self, Purpose (yours and your reader's), Audience, Code, and Experience all influence organization, make sure you've done a thorough preview before attempting serious organizing.

The Process Of Organizing

Step 1. Have your Previewing firmly in mind.

Step 2. Fire your anchor for an organized state of mind. Use your Designer State Worksheet as a reminder, if you need to.

Step 3. Use an outline or some other visual structuring device.

Questions About Your Organization

- Do I have a very clear Preview?
- Am I in the best state I can be in to organize this material?
- Do I need to fill in a Designer State Worksheet to help me?
- Do I need to anchor this state, keeping me feeling and thinking in my most organized fashion while I decide on or develop my organization for this project?

- What kind of organizational pattern would be most useful for my reader's Purpose?
- What kind of organizational pattern would be most useful for my own Purpose?
- Does one of the classical organization patterns stand out clearly as the best choice for this material:
    Chronological narration?
    Spatial description?
    Illustration with examples, metaphor, or analogy?
    Comparison and contrast?
    Classification?
    A process pattern?
    Cause-effect?
    Definition?
- Do I need to "chunk up" or "chunk down" my information to get the organizing started?

- Have I, or others, ever successfully organized this or similar information before? Could I do it that way again?

- Can I outline (or diagram or chart) my information ?
- Does the outline (or diagram) look logical?
- Does all the information fit in some logical place in the outline?
    Is the information that doesn't have a place essential?
    Is there some relationship between parts that have been left out?
    What is the relationship of the left-out information to the main ideas in the outline?
- Are there any empty spots in the outline (or diagram)?
    Where can I get the information needed (back to Experience)?

- Have I chosen an organizational pattern I am comfortable with?
- Do any feelings I have about it make me uneasy or hesitant to write?

  Will this make my work too difficult?

- Does thinking about how I have organized this material produce a worthwhile state for me to be in while I write?
- Does it make me want to get right into the Writing phase?

  Would it help me to pick an alternative organizational pattern to use while I write, just to get through, and then reorganize later?

- Do I need to fill out a Designer State Worksheet to help me at this point?
- Do I need to anchor a state of confidence and clarity about how I have organized this material to help me continue in the writing process?

WRITING

Remember that Writing is only the middle stage of the whole writing process. Its Purpose is to get the information out of your head (and any other sources) and onto paper in one place, to make it visible externally and ready for evaluation.

The Process Of Writing

Step 1. Have your Previewing firmly in mind.

Step 2. Have your outline or other visual structuring device in view.

Step 3. Prepare physically. That is, sit down with paper and pen, or turn your computer on, etc.

Step 4. Fire your anchor for a state of compulsion. Use your Designer State Worksheet for Compulsion as a reminder, if you need to.

Questions About Your Writing

- Am I in the best state I can be to write?
- Do I feel compelled to begin and keep going to the end?
- Do I need to fill out a Designer State Worksheet to help me?
- Do I need to anchor this state to help me maintain it while I write?

- Do I have all the tools I need to write?
- Is my setting conducive to writing?
    If not, is my compulsion strong enough to compensate?

- How quickly can I get all my information externalized in one place?
- Do I have "best" methods, both internal and external, for getting ideas onto paper or the screen?

- What do I imagine (pictures, sounds, words, feelings) the writing of this will be like?
- Do I have any discomfort about proceeding?
    Anything that will slow me down or get in the way?
    Do I need to change this before going further?

EVALUATING

Evaluating will be done in phases, alternating with Revising, so that you won't be making unnecessary adjustments to your text.

The Process Of Evaluating

Phase One: Content from Your Own Point of View
Step 1. Using your organizing tool (outline, diagram, flow chart, etc.), check to be sure you have included all the information you intended. Make notes about what still needs to be inserted if you find omissions.

Step 2. Take on the role you developed for your Self in the Previewing stage and read what you've written, making sure that what you've written matches what you intended to say and that you've maintained a consistent image. Make notes about any changes needed.

Step 3. Go to Revising and make whatever adjustments are needed in your content at this point.

Step 4. In First Position, as your Self, evaluate your manuscript again with your Audience in mind. If your Audience response is less than you'd like at any point, make notes.

Phase Two: Content from Your Reader's Point of View
Step 5. Go to Second Position, assuming the role of your Audience. As you read and evaluate, make notes about your feelings and other responses.

Step 6. Go to Revising and make whatever adjustments are indicated by your notes from Steps 4 and 5.

Phase Three: Structure and Style
Step 7. Check paragraphs for unity and coherence, length, and transition.

Step 8. Go to Revising and make whatever adjustments are indicated.

Step 9. Check sentences for grammar, mechanics, word choice, variety and length.

Step 10. Go to Revising and make whatever adjustments are indicated.

Step 11. Check overall layout and design for structural markers (headings, etc.), graphic support and practical accessibility of information.

Step 12. Go to Revising and make whatever adjustments are indicated.

Phase Four: Proofseeing

Step 13. Distance yourself from your content and Purpose and see what is on the page, looking for surface errors like typographical errors, punctuation mistakes, etc.

Step 14. Go to Revising and make whatever corrections are necessary.

or

Speed your finished writing on its way.

Questions About Your Evaluating

Phase One: Content from Your Own Point of View

- Have I gotten all the content down on paper?

    Have I omitted anything that should be added?

    Are there any errors in the content?

- Did I get the material down in the way I intended it to be organized?

    Are all related ideas in the same place?

    Are ideas sequenced properly?

    Are sections, or groups of ideas, properly labeled or identified in some way?

- Did I maintain my role throughout the entire project?

    Have I marked any inconsistent spots for revision?

- Does what I've written actually reflect the ideas I had in mind?

    Have I accomplished what I set out to do?

    Will this achieve my Purpose in writing?

Phase Two: Content from Your Reader's Point of View

- Can I imagine watching my Audience read what I have written?

    Do I like what I see?

    Would I want it to be different in some way? How?

- If I could hear my Audience talking back to me, what might they be saying?

    How would I feel about their responses?

    Have I accomplished my goals?

    Am I getting the responses I want?

    Do I want different responses? What?

- Can I imagine myself as a member of my Audience?
- In Second Position, as my intended reader, how do I respond to this writing?
    Does the writing accomplish the writer's Purpose?
    Does it accomplish my Purpose as a reader?
    Am I puzzled anywhere as I read?
    Do I need more clarification, information, or examples?
    Is the Code appropriate for me?
    Am I bored in any place as I read this? Why?
    Does it leave any of my questions unanswered?
    Is that all right?

Phase Three: Structure and Style
- Have I checked paragraph structure?
    Is there a new paragraph each time there is a shift in topic?
    Are the paragraphs short enough to give my reader "eye relief"?
    Is the topic of the paragraph clear (topic sentence or other unifying clues)?
    Do all the sentences in the paragraph clearly relate to the topic?
    Did I make adequate and smooth transitions between paragraphs and ideas?

- Have I checked sentence structure?
    Are my sentences grammatically and mechanically correct?
    Do I need professional assistance?
    Do I have enough variety in sentence style and length?
    Have I used active voice wherever possible?

- Have I checked word choice?
    Have I eliminated unnecessary jargon and empty words?
    Have I defined technical, specialized, or complex terms?
    Have I used non-sexist, inclusive language?

- Is the overall layout the best it can be?
     Is the relation of parts clear and logical?
     Have I used graphic aids (pictures, charts, etc.) everywhere they would be useful?
          Are these clearly labeled?
          Are they integrated into the text?
          Do I need professional help with graphics?

- Have I carefully and properly given references and credit to all my sources of information?
- Have I obtained permission to use the material?

Phase Four: Proofseeing
- Have I carefully checked the final manuscript for errors?
- Do I need a partner to help me proof this manuscript?
- Do I have the necessary skills to spot any errors?
- Do I need professional help?

REVISING

Revising will be done in stages alternating with Evaluating.

The Process Of Revising

Phase One: Content from Your Own Point of View
Step 1. Return to the Previewing stage and make sure the context is still appropriate.

Step 2. Go through Organizing again if necessary.

Step 3. Return to the Writing stage and the appropriate compulsion state. Make the content changes indicated by your evaluation, without taking time for further evaluation or stylistic changes.

Phase Two: Content from Your Reader's Point of View
Step 4. Repeat Steps 1-3, using the notes from your second phase of evaluating.

Phase Three: Structure and Style

Step 5. Return to the Writing stage and the appropriate compulsion state. Make the structural and stylistic changes indicated by your evaluation.

Phase Four: Proofseeing

Step 6. Carefully check the surface of the manuscript (see, don't read) for grammar, spelling, punctuation, etc. errors.

Step 7. Repeat Step 6 if any re-typing or copying is done.

Questions about Your Revising

- Do I have notes from my evaluation in or along with my first draft, so that I can easily revise what I've done?
- Do I know what to change and how?
    - Do I need to get more information about what is needed?
    - Do I need professional help with accomplishing the changes?

- Am I ready to go back into my state of Writing compulsion again?
- Can I do it smoothly, comfortably and quickly?

- Have I made use of all my evaluation notes?
- Am I ready to cycle back through the evaluating and revising hierarchy?

- How could I make it more attractive to the reader?
- Do I know what criteria I will use to decide when I have made this project as good as it can possibly be, or as good as it needs to be?
    - Am I willing to put forth the effort needed to reach that goal?
    - Do I need another state to get me Finished?

Bibliography

Annotated Bibliography

This bibliography makes no pretense of being complete or definitive. It represents books and other resources we've personally found useful and enjoyable, and we recommend them to our friends. Our selections were influenced by personal prejudice, immediate availability and friendship. They are grouped in three categories: NLP-based books, books on writing, and other helpful resources.

Neuro-Linguistic Programming

Bagley, Dan S., and Edward Reese: *Beyond Selling.*
Cupertino, Calif.: Meta Publications, 1987.
> An introductory book on sales using NLP techniques. Incudes a very thorough section on establishing rapport and some abbreviated information on techniques useful throughout the sales cycle.

Bandler, Richard: *Using Your Brain—For A Change.*
Moab, Utah: Real People Press, 1985.
> A complete introduction to sub-modalities, taken from workshop material presented by one of the developers of NLP. It is aimed at self help, but provides useful insights for a variety of situations, including handling blocks and creating useful states of consciousness.

Bandler, Richard and John Grinder: *The Structure Of Magic, Vol I.*
Palo Alto, Calif.: Science and Behavior Books, 1975.
> The first book on Neuro-Linguistic Programming continues to be one of the greatest analyses of the use of language. Though it is aimed at psychotherapeutic uses of language, the information in it is valuable for anyone who is also a professional communicator. The language model presented is outstanding for insuring clarity in language and communication.

Dilts, Robert: *Applications Of Neuro-Linguistic Programming: A Practical Guide To Communication, Learning, And Change.*
Cupertino, Calif.: Meta Publications, 1983.
> A series of articles, all written by one of the original contributors to NLP. These cover a wide range of topics including the use of NLP in business and educational settings and in creative writing.

Dilts, Robert B., Todd Epstein, and Robert W.Dilts: *Tools For Dreamers: Strategies For Creativity And The Structure Of Innovation.*
Cupertino, Calif: Meta Publications, 1991.
> A long-awaited text on using NLP technology to enhance creativity. Includes exercises and concepts that can be used by anyone to boost creativity and the ability to be innovative. Interviews with highly creative people are accompanied by an explanation of their strategies.

Gordon, David: *Therapeutic Metaphors: Helping Others Through The Looking Glass.*
Cupertino, Calif.: Meta Publications, 1978.
> How to tell stories to help people change. It includes models for the construction of metaphors that relate directly to the person hearing the story. The concepts are applicable to many forms of writing and will help the writer in carefully considering Audience in new and powerful ways.

Jacobson, Sid: *Meta-Cation: Prescriptions For Some Ailing Educational Processes.*
Cupertino, Calif.: Meta Publications, 1983.
> The first book in a three-volume series on NLP applied to the field and processes of education. It may be the best, and clearest, introduction to the technology of NLP, complete with exercises designed to teach the basic skills. Includes thorough discussions of representational systems and anchoring, as well as a good description of how to apply these skills in communicating in a teaching environment.

Jacobson, Sid: *Meta-Cation, Vol.II: New Improved Formulas For Thinking About Thinking.*
Cupertino, Calif.: Meta Publications, 1986.
> The second of three volumes on NLP applied to education. It presents an overview of the NLP model in a hierarchical framework. Included are good descriptions of the use of sub-modalities in developing states of consciousness and applying these states to specific tasks.

Richardson, Jerry: *The Magic Of Rapport: How You Can Gain Personal Power In Any Situation.*
Cupertino, Calif: Meta Publications, 1987.
> Another very introductory book on using NLP to establish and enhance rapport with other people. Includes many tips on getting along with people, even in difficult situations, as well as avoiding conflict in graceful ways.

Books On Writing

Burnett, Rebecca: *Technical Communication. (3rd edition)*
Belmont, Calif.: Wadsworth, Inc., 1994.
> Thorough textbook, including writing with other people. Takes advantage of current research in how people learn and write.

Hills, Rust: *Writing In General And The Short Story In Particular: An Informal Textbook.*
Boston: Houghton Mifflin, 1977.
> A wealth of information on most aspects of how to construct stories by an experienced fiction editor, collected in, as the title suggests, an informal manner. It contains so much information on plot, character, point of view, and quality writing that it seems a nearly inexhaustible set of reminders for anyone writing fiction.

Hodges, John C: *The Harbrace College Handbook.*
New York: Harcourt, Brace, Jovanovich, 1989.
> A good all-purpose reference for grammar, mechanics, and style. It's due for a revision soon, but this edition or any of the previous ones (check used book stores) will do just fine.

Hughes, Elaine: *Writing from the Inner Self.*
New York: HarperCollins, 1991.
> Wonderful ways to encourage yourself to say what's on your mind and in your heart.

Knight, Damon: *Creating Short Fiction.*
Cincinnati: Writer's Digest Books, 1981.
> A structured approach to short story writing, by one of the great science fiction writers. It presents a guide to most elements of short story writing, complete with exercises to develop your skill. Especially interesting are the sections on plot and structure, but all of the material is invaluable to the writer of short fiction.

Murray, Donald: *The Craft Of Revision.*
New York: Holt Rinehart and Winston, 1991.
> Compatible with the POWER Process, this book goes into more detail about revising the mechanical elements of your text. Take his advice, but use the more efficient POWER hierarchy.

Thomas E., and Donald H. Cunningham: *How To Write For The World Of Work. (5th edition)*
Orlando, Fla.: Holt, Rinehart and Winston, Inc., 1994.
> Textbook focuses on "transactional" writing, writing intended to get something done.

Pickett, Nell Ann, and Ann Laster: *Technical English: Reading, Writing, And Speaking. (7th edition)*
New York: Harper & Row, 1996.
> A good introduction to technical writing, with lots of plan sheets to guide each kind of writing task.

Rico, Gabrielle Lusser: *Writing The Natural Way: Using Right Brain Techniques To Release Your Expressive Powers.*
Los Angeles: J. P. Tarcher, Inc., 1983.
> If you want to write but think you don't have anything to say, this book will take you through techniques for discovering your ideas.

The Science Fiction Writers of America: *Writing And Selling Science Fiction.*
Cincinnati: Writer's Digest Books, 1976.
> A series of articles by top science fiction writers covering many aspects of the field. It includes fine articles on characterization, dialogue, language, speculation and other important features of science fiction writing, in addition to articles on marketing and selling your work.

Silverman, Jay, Elaine Hughes, and Diana Roberts Wienbroer: *Rules of Thumb: A Guide For Writers.*
New York: McGraw-Hill, 1990.
> A user-friendly collection of good advice on the rules governing English.

Stoddard, Alexander: *Gift Of A Letter.*
New York: Avon Books, 1990.
> Brings her consciousness of beautiful living to letter writing. If you procrastinate on notes, this book will inspire you to let your letters enrich others' lives as well as your own.

Zinsser, William: *On Writing Well: An Informal Guide To Writing Nonfiction. (4th edition)*
New York: Harper Collins, 1990.
> A classic text and a must for anyone who wants to write quality non-fiction. The sections on style and word usage and simplicity are unsurpassed. Also included are tips on many kinds of writing including sports, criticism, humor, interviewing, and more. An absolutely invaluable book.

Other Helpful Resources

The Association of Professional Communication Consultants.
This organization can refer you to a writing consultant in your area. Send your referral request for the specific kind of help you need to APCC's international headquarters at 3924 South Troost, Tulsa, OK 74105.

Authors Guild, Inc.
330 West 42nd Street, New York, NY 10036
Telephone: 212-563-5904
The Authors Guild (of which Sid is a member) is a large group of book authors, organized around the issues, trends and difficulties of publishing their work. You must be a published author to belong, but they provide tremendous guidance to those who do. They also have a service for reviewing contracts and providing other vital business guidelines for authors. They participate in legal debate and are involved in advising legislators on issues of publication in the United States and elsewhere.

Sylvia K. Burack, Ed.: *The Writer's Handbook.*
Boston: The Writer, Inc., 1991.
Short pieces of advice from writers on a wide range of topics and current market specifications.

Dilts, Robert: *The NeuroLink.*
NeuroLink International, 343 Soquel Avenue, #334, Santa Cruz, CA. 95062. Telephone: (408) 483-5679. Fax: (408) 438-6649. Internet: http://www.scruz.net/~rdilts/neurowb.htm.
A multi-channel biofeedback device and software (either Macintosh or IBM-compatible) that allows your computer to help you adjust your physical, mental, and/or emotional state. You can use it to assist in reaching the states we suggest for the POWER Process, using exactly the same procedures, or expand the applications to controlling your blood pressure. You can also save the physiological information about each state you design and let your computer provide anchors for each state. If you are a computer user, the NeuroLink is a great additional tool.

Goldin, Stephen and Kathleen Sky. *The Business Of Being A Writer.*
New York: Carroll & Graf Publishers, Inc., 1982.
>   This is a book by two experienced science fiction writers who have
>   gone through the pains and successes of selling their work. It is a
>   thorough examination of what it means to be a professional writer,
>   from considering how and what to write, to marketing and selling
>   your work, to dealing with agents and publishers, handling
>   contracts, and even keeping records and doing your taxes. A very
>   good overview of the profession.

Goldfarb, Ronald, and Gail E. Ross: *The Writer's Lawyer.*
New York: Times Books (a division of Random House), 1989.
>   Offers legal advice ranging from libel defense to contracts.

Schultz, Dodi, Ed. for the American Society of Journalists and Authors:
Tools Of The Writer's Trade.
New York: HarperCollins, 1990.
>   Professional writers share their opinions of their tools, from
>   computers and answer machines to books, copy services, and
>   publishing helps.

Sorenson, George: *Writing For The Corporate Market: How To Make
Big Money Freelancing For Business.*
Denver: Mid-Lift Press, 1990.
>   Good advice on getting started and what to look out for.

Williams, Becky Hall, Ed.: **1998** *The Writer's Market: Where To Sell
What You Write.*
Cincinnati: Writer's Digest Books. Published annually.
>   Many professional writers consider this reference book as important
>   a tool as a dictionary or thesaurus. It is an encyclopedia of all of the
>   major markets—magazines, book publishers, greeting card
>   publishers, and so on—that buy the work of writers, updated
>   annually. Includes editor's names, addresses, subject and style
>   preferences, some specific instructions on submitting to that
>   company, and what they pay as well as much more valuable infor-
>   mation. It also includes advice articles by writers and editors, an
>   enormous number of tips for authors, and profiles of successful
>   people in the field. Companion books include markets for photogra-
>   phers, script writers, fiction writers, and more.

Yudkin, Marcia: *Freelance Writing For Magazines And Newspapers:
Breaking In Without Selling Out.*
>   Includes basics on structuring and focusing articles, but emphasizes
>   the nitty gritty of getting them accepted for publication.

The Anglo-American Book Company Ltd
Crown Buildings,
Bancyfelin,
Carmarthen, SA33 5ND
Wales.
Telephone: 01267 211880 / 211886

We trust you enjoyed this title from our range of bestselling books for professional and general readership. All our authors are professionals of many years' experience, and all are highly respected in their own field. We choose our books with care for their content and character, and for the value of their contribution of both new and updated material to their particular field. Here is a list of all our other publications.

Figuring Out People: *Design Engineering With Meta-Programs*
  by Bob G. Bodenhamer & L. Michael Hall   Paperback £12.99

Gold Counselling™: *A Practical Psychology With NLP*
  by Georges Philips   Paperback £14.99

Grieve No More, Beloved: *The Book Of Delight*
  by Ormond McGill   Hardback   £9.99

Influencing With Integrity: *Management Skills For Communication And Negotiation*
  by Genie Z Laborde   Paperback £12.50

Living Organisations: *Beyond The Learning Organisation*
  by Lex McKee   Hardback   £14.99

The New Encyclopedia Of Stage Hypnotism
  by Ormond McGill   Hardback   £29.99

The POWER Process: *An NLP Approach To Writing*
  by Dixie Elise Hickman & Sid Jacobson   Paperback £12.99

Scripts & Strategies In Hypnotherapy
  by Roger P. Allen   Hardback   £19.99

Seeing The Unseen: *A Past Life Revealed Through Hypnotic Regression*
  by Ormond McGill   Paperback £12.99

Solution States: *A Course In Solving Problems In Business Using NLP*
  by Sid Jacobson   Paperback £12.99

The Spirit Of NLP: *The Process, Meaning And Criteria For Mastering NLP*
  by L. Michael Hall   Paperback £12.99

Time-Lining: *Patterns For Adventuring In "Time"*
  by Bob G. Bodenhamer & L. Michael Hall   Paperback £14.99